"Symptoms to Watch for in Your Dog *is a valuable addition to a dog owners' library and a big help to ensure that dogs receive timely medical care. At the other end of the leash from the dog is a human. Humans are the gatekeepers of their dogs' health. The more aware they are of their needs, the better off the dogs will be. The experiences of a dog owner who has been through many health issues with their dogs can help guide others towards getting appropriate care for their dogs. An average dog owner may only have 1, 2 or 3 dogs in their entire lives. Knowing what is normal and abnormal can take exposure to hundreds of dogs. This book helps fill in that missing experience.*"

Dr. Rae Worden – Fergus Veterinary Hospital, aka Jasmine's vet

"*Life just became easier for dog owners/parents.* Symptoms to Watch for in Your Dog *truly leaves no stone unturned and more importantly, teaches HOW to advocate for your dog. Knowledge is power, and this important new book provides the tools to "read" their dogs and get them to the Vet pronto when necessary. All the tools are there.* Symptoms to Watch For *flows in a logical easy to read format, both instructive and exhaustively thorough. Every pet owner, indeed every Dog Behavior Consultant, will want this book. Practicing the latter Profession for years taught me that dog illness was very frequently at the root of a change in behavior. I applaud Jana Rade, an expert in all matters of dog health, for concisely and succinctly making important information available to pet owners in* Symptoms to Watch For. *I've know Jana for years via Social Media, and it has been my pleasure to preview the outstanding* Symptoms to Watch For.*"

Leslie Clifton – PMCT (Pat Miller Certified Trainer)
CPDT-KA (Certified Pet Dog Trainer-Knowledge Assessed)
Dog Behavior Consultant
Retired DogSmith Dog Training Professional

"Jana is a passionate dog mom. Her passion for her dogs has turned her pet parenting into a quest to understand and assist them at every turn of their ever-evolving medical needs. Jana has become a learned student of pet nutrition, orthopedics, training, behavior, and all things dog. She has assimilated her experiences into a book to help other dog lovers learn about how to best care for their dogs. Her no-frills, straight-talk advice is easy to read, pet parent-friendly and simplifies the often overly superfluous scientific jargon that is difficult to process into accessible, meaningful and helpful dog health information. It is through her years of research, personal experience and dedication to her Rottie kids that the rest of the pet parents around the world will benefit."

Dr. Krista Magnifico – Founder and Chief Creative Officer at Pawbly and Owner at Jarrettsville Vet Center

"In her quest to learn everything possible about dog health, Jana Rade has become a master at detecting symptoms that need to be addressed by a veterinary health care professional. Her book is a valuable resource for canine parents everywhere. Take comfort that she will be your guiding light in identifying, understanding and assessing problem areas. Your dog's well-being depends on it."

Susan E. Davis – PT Animal Physical Therapist and Author

"Symptoms to Watch for in Your Dog is an excellent guide for first-time or long-time dog lovers. I've had a dog in my life since I was born. I've written about veterinary medicine and pet care for many years, and I still learned new things – especially about dog poop. Do yourself and your dog a favor. Read this book."*

Roxanne Hawn – author of *Heart Dog: Surviving the Loss of Your Canine Soul Mate* and dog blog Champion of My Heart

"Symptoms To Watch For In Your Dog is an eye-opening journey through the veterinary system and how it affects your dog's health. It demonstrates the realities and importance of taking control of your dog's medical care. This book is a must-read for those who love their pets and wish to take a pro-active and productive role in their dog's physical well-being."

Norma Jeanne Laurette – IPDTA-CDT, Dog Trainer/Behaviour Therapist & Author

"The knowledge Jana Rade has acquired through her years of owning dogs and communicating with dog owners in social media has given her unique insight as to what pet owners worry about. Symptoms to Watch For in Your Dog can help you to not only figure out when to seek out treatment but also how to choose a veterinarian who will communicate with you in a way that makes you feel comfortable, and that addresses your concerns. This book has made being a dog parent so much easier. Even with my 20+ years as a dog owner and member of the veterinary community, I found the book helpful in so many areas. Dog parents should add this book to their arsenal for care for their dog."

Kristi Hauta – Former Veterinary Technician and Practice Manager

"Dogs love us in amazing ways. My own dogs show me this every day. But our faithful family members can't tell us what is wrong when they're not feeling well. That's why this book is so important. With solid advice such as which symptoms you should never ignore, and how to tell when your dog is in pain, this thorough book is a must-have resource for every pet parent."

Peggy Frezon – Contributing Editor All Creatures magazine, author of *Faithfully Yours, the amazing bond between us and the animals we love.*

"Jana's book taught me that I know and love my dogs best, and that's why it's my job to be their advocate. It's up to me to find the best vet but also to speak up, ask questions, trust my gut and seek a second (or third) opinion if something doesn't add up.

I've always found Jana's writing to be a voice of reason, both on her blog "Dawg Business" and now in her book. Symptoms to Watch for in Your Dog reminds me to pay attention when something seems "off" with a pet and to appreciate the value of a compassionate vet who listens."

Lindsay Stordahl – writer, dog walker, rescue volunteer

"Everyone who is a dog owner has a responsibility to be a health advocate for their dog. Being able to tell when your dog is sick is at the foundation of caring for their health.

There is a lot of dog health information available, but a lot of it is full of medical jargon and difficult for a dog owner to understand sufficiently to make good decisions.

Over several years Jana compiled a wealth of information to put together an owner-to-owner book that would provide understandable and accurate information on what symptoms your dog may exhibit, and what these symptoms could mean."

Jerry Rade

"I'll never look at my dogs the same way after reading, "Symptoms to Watch for in Your Dog." Jana Rade gives the reader a panoply of symptoms to look for when your best friend might not be feeling tip-top. Based on her personal experiences and with input from top veterinarians, Jana left with me with one overriding thought regarding my dogs' health. "When in doubt, err on the side of caution."

Bob Poole – author of "Listen First – Sell Later" and "Six Dozen Doughnuts"

Symptoms
to Watch for in your
DOG

How to Tell if Your Dog Is Sick
and What to Do Next

JANA RADE
Edited by Dr. Joanna Paul BSc BVSc

Symptoms to Watch for in Your Dog: How to Tell if Your Dog Is Sick and What to Do Next

ISBN: 978-0-9952474-0-6
First edition. 2017

Edited by: Dr. Joanna Paul BSc BVSc
Design and layout: Jana Rade

Published by Dawg Business Publications

Disclaimer: The information provided in this book is designed to provide helpful information about potential symptoms you might observe in your dog. It is not meant to be used, nor should it be used, to diagnose or treat any medical condition. For diagnosis or treatment please consult your veterinarian. References are provided for informational purposes only.

This book does not list all the symptoms your dog might be experiencing and it is not intended as a substitute for veterinary care. Its purpose is to hopefully teach you to be a health advocate for your dog and understand when your dog needs to see a veterinarian.

Your job as a dog parent is to:

- find a good veterinarian
- recognize when something isn't right with your dog
- know when and how quickly to see a veterinarian
- know when to seek a second opinion

To Jasmine, my heart dog, who taught me everything.

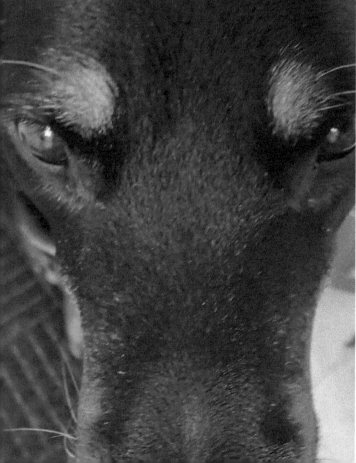

The Dogs behind My Learning Curve

Sometimes you get that one dog in your life who gives you a lifetime of education. Jasmine and her health challenges provided me with a crash course in dog health advocacy. I still remember one vet telling me that not all bad things always happen and if they do, not to the same dog. Jasmine did not get that memo. It would probably take a hundred dogs to learn all I did with her.

I made my mistakes, the biggest and most common one being not knowing any better and not standing up for her in spite of my gut telling me that there was more to things than met the eye.

I still remember the first time I read the back of a treats package. We started buying them because they looked good, smelled good, and Jasmine liked them. It wasn't until they must have changed their formula and the treats suddenly looked, felt and smelled wrong when I turned the bag to look at the ingredients. The package went straight in the trash, and I have examined the contents of everything I bought for my dogs since.

I remember how unhappy I was with the lack of satisfactory explanation and resolution of Jasmine's continuing digestive issues. And yet I accepted the "sensitive stomach" diagnosis and did nothing about it.

I remember how desperate I got when Jasmine would spend night after night pacing around, panting, and being miserable, again with no explanation. Even though I did make up my mind that enough was enough and I wasn't leaving the vet's office until it got figured out and resolved.

The vet did come up with a desperate theory which needed to be either confirmed or ruled out. He figured that the problem was low thyroid hormone. Jasmine indeed did have an underactive thyroid. She also put on some weight which went under our and the vet's radar.

But he tested for it poorly which I didn't know at the time. I also didn't know that other problems in the body could affect thyroid hormone levels.

As soon as Jasmine started getting thyroid supplement, she did start dropping some of the extra weight. For a short while, it seemed that it solved her other problems as well. But it did not.

The first time I decided to take charge was when Jasmine was diagnosed with a ruptured knee ligament, and her vet told us she needed TPLO surgery. After looking up what the heck it was, we really didn't like it. I started researching other options. And what do you know, there were other options even though we were only presented with the one.

Health challenge after health challenge I was learning to take charge of Jasmine's health. Learning to tell when something was wrong. Finding a good vet. Getting second opinions. Working through the diagnosis. Considering and discussing all treatments.

Realizing how much better I could have done for Jasmine if I knew better from the start, I started sharing our journey and experiences online. That is Jasmine's legacy.

Learning from one's mistakes is great. Being able to learn from somebody else's mistakes is even better.

We adopted Cookie few months after Jasmine's passing to honor her memory by saving another Rottie. I wanted a healthy one this time. Cookie was a year and a half old, sweet, lovely and appeared perfectly healthy.

The second day after we adopted her she became fully lame on her left hind leg. I couldn't believe it. Did she really manage to bust her knee within 48 hours of being with us?

That time we got off lucky. The knee was fine; it was a piece of porcupine quill buried deep in Cookie's foot. Or at least that's what we thought. In retrospect, I wonder whether two things happened at one time, and one got missed in the process. You can be chasing down one problem while another slips under the radar.

Once we took care of that, it became apparent that Cookie was going to follow in Jasmine's footstep in every conceivable way, including going through the rest of the vet textbook.

So here I am again. But this time, I know how to do things.

Our boy dogs had been relatively healthy with a *normal* amount of health challenges you'd expect to run into having a dog. Even then there were things to learn.

The most important lesson I've learned with Roxy, our first Rotty, is compassion. I learned what it is like having a sick dog and no money to do anything about it.

Sometimes I sit there wondering why I couldn't have *just a healthy dog*. Hubby tells me I got these girls because they needed me. And perhaps people who find our stories needed that too. So I do my best to make sure that what we've been through helps as many dogs as possible.

And then there are all the family member's and friends' dogs whose journeys and challenges I had the privilege to be part of.

Contents

Advocating for your Dog's Health

Preface

I have asked some of my veterinary friends what they consider the 10 most important symptoms to watch for in our dogs. To summarize their responses: "When anything about the dog changes." That is the bottom line.

Here is what they had to say:

Having just experienced a tragedy that still has my friend's children crying themselves to sleep, I am compelled to give just one answer to this question—LOSS OF APPETITE.

Recently my friend was babysitting a senior dog for her close friend on vacation. Less than 24 hours into their time together, the dog became lethargic and began vomiting. Rapid breathing followed. My friend texted me a video of the dog and we walked through a crude exam by phone. My heart sank because intuitively I knew this was serious.

My friend rushed the dog to a local vet who diagnosed a large mass of the spleen on physical exam.

The poor dog was a time bomb for bleeding to death internally, and she was too weak even to get up. After communicating with the dog's owner several times via phone, it was determined unanimously that the kindest thing for the suffering dog was euthanasia. It was a tragic, traumatic outcome, and completely blindsided my friend and her family.

However, in discussing the unfolding situation with the out-of-state owner, it came to light that the dog had not been eating normally for weeks. The lady had naively ignored this symptom, which in most dogs is a major red flag.

If your dog has an unexplainable/uncharacteristic decrease or cessation of appetite that lasts for more than one meal, please contact your veterinarian immediately.

—Dr. Julie Buzby, Dr. Buzby's ToeGrips for Dogs

I have had clients come in to see me because the hair on their dog is going a different way in a spot than it did a couple of months ago - NOT an exaggeration!

When should you bring your dog to the vet:

- *The obvious, such as bleeding, gaping wounds, loss of consciousness, multiple seizures, obvious broken limbs, difficulty breathing, paralysis, or painful cries dictate a need to get to the vet ASAP.*

Other symptoms that may not be as obvious to some people but do warrant a visit to your vet include:

- *Digestive disorders: Vomiting more than once in a 24 hour period, diarrhea for more than 24 hours, not eating for more than 24 hours, blood in the stool*

- *Respiratory disorders: Coughing, sneezing, nasal or eye discharge for more than 3-4 days, excessive panting when the dog is at rest, and it's not hot, any labored breathing*
- *Eye disorders: Anything relating to the eye calls for a visit to the vet within 24 hours*
- *Urinary tract disorders: Straining to urinate, blood in the urine or having accidents in the house, drinking excessively and/or urinating excessively*
- *Musculoskeletal disorders: Not being able to raise or turn the head, wobbly or weak in the hind legs, not putting weight on a leg, limping for more than three days or a limp that gets worse instead of better*
- *General: Restlessness, not able to sleep, depressed and not wanting to play, hiding and not wanting to be around family, a significant change in behavior*

I am sure I have missed some other concerns that would require a trip to the vet, but I did purposely leave out a spot of hair going in a different direction than it once was. It's fine if you bring your dog to a vet for an issue such as that, but it is not an immediate concern and certainly would not be in a top 10 of what to watch out for.

—Dr. Daniel Beatty, DVM, Dog Kinetics

Top 10 symptoms owners should watch for in their dogs:

- *Unintentional weight loss*
- *Increased water consumption*
- *Changes in urinary habits—either frequency or volume*
- *Vomiting: Chronic vomiting is not normal. Pets that vomit once or twice a week, off and on need to be checked out*
- *Coughing*
- *Sneezing or nasal discharge*
- *Bad breath: This is most often caused by dental disease but could also be an indication of systemic illness*

- *Red ears or smell coming from the ears*
- *Hair loss*
- *Changes in bowel habits*

—Dr. Keith Niesenbaum, VMD, New York,
Crawford Dog and Cat Hospital

- *Changes in volume of water drunk*
- *Changes in volume of urine produced*
- *Gain or loss of weight*
- *Unexplained lumps*
- *Vomiting*
- *Diarrhea*
- *Blood visible anywhere*
- *Gain or loss of appetite*
- *PAIN or the suggestion of PAIN anywhere*
- *ANY issue the veterinarian says is abnormal or requires monitoring*

—Dr. Rae Worden, DVM, Ontario, Fergus Veterinary Hospital

- *Vomiting*
- *Diarrhea*
- *Coughing*
- *Sneezing*
- *Not eating or decreased appetite*
- *Lethargic*
- *Behavioral change: Any change in the dog's normal behavior*
- *Acting painful or limping*
- *Shaking head*
- *Increased thirst and urination*

When I see a client, these are questions that we ask regarding their pet so that we can properly diagnose and treat what is wrong. If your dog has any of the above symptoms, you should contact your veterinarian.

—Dr. Anna M. Coffin, DVM, Guthrie Pet Hospital

- *Difficulty breathing or any change in respiratory patterns*
- *Vomiting*
- *Diarrhea or other alterations in bowel movements*
- *Abnormal urinary patterns or appearance of urine*
- *Water consumption changes*
- *Decreased appetite*
- *Lethargy*
- *Exercise intolerance*
- *Lameness: Limping, not being able to go up/down stairs or on/off elevated surfaces, etc.*
- *General behavior changes: Hiding, aggression, not wanting to be held/touched*

—Dr. Patrick Mahaney, Los Angeles, The Daily Vet

Most people know to watch out for symptoms such as vomiting, diarrhea, and lethargy.

I will mention 10 important symptoms that people are more likely to ignore. If you observe any of these, veterinary visit is warranted:

- *Increased thirst*
- *Increased appetite*
- *Diminished (narrower) urine stream*
- *Decreased stamina (exercise intolerance)*
- *Feeling more bony prominences when petting your dog*
- *Increased panting*
- *Eating normal amount of food, but taking longer to do so*
- *Change in behavior: clinginess, grouchiness, etc.*
- *Change in texture of the coat*
- *Unexplained change in body weight*

—Dr. Nancy Kay, DVM, Speaking for Spot

- *Shortness of breath or breathing difficulty:* People often miss this subtle, slow onset as lethargy, or panting. A pet with an extended head and neck, open mouth, or abdominal involvement in moving air, is having difficulty breathing. This is a medical emergency.
- *Distended abdomen:* Most pet parents don't notice this either, but it is one of the most important clues in bloat, which requires immediate surgical intervention.
- *Gagging, retching, attempting to vomit with or without producing vomit or liquid from the mouth:* This is also another sign of bloat or an intestinal obstruction. Both require immediate veterinary care and intervention.
- *Panting:* Excessive panting can be difficult to distinguish from ordinary panting, but your dog's internal temperature can climb quickly and become life threatening. A panting dog who becomes quiet, recumbent, and lethargic is in some cases a dying dog.
- *Excessive chewing:* Some people think that having lots of rawhides, toys, chews, etc. around will keep their pet from becoming bored, but in some cases, these dogs learn to become fixated on oral stimuli, which perpetuates more chewing, and chewing on objects that are not safe. If your dog is an excessive chewer I worry about intestinal obstructions. We have seen 2 and 3-year-old dogs undergo multiple exploratory surgeries. Think about whether your pet is bored. Dogs need exercise, mental stimulation, and a safe, happy, engaging environment. Feed that, not the stomach.
- *Persistent lameness:* If your dog is limping and it either becomes more severe OR persists it is time for an examination, and at some point, it is time for an x-ray, or even serial x-rays to identify cancer, osteoarthritis, and other possible soft tissue or orthopedic conditions. The earlier these are diagnosed, the better the chance of successful treatment options.
- *Obesity:* Many pet parents don't realize how those pounds creep up. Because they are with their dog every day they don't recognize that their furry friend is packing on pounds that can lead to diabetes, cancer, osteoarthritis, other diseases, and premature

death. Obesity is an epidemic in the USA for both pet and their parents. This is a preventable disease!

- *Head shaking, licking paws, scratching... and all of the rest of the ways our pets try to tell us that their skin is bothering them: All of these clinical signs tell me that your pet has a struggle with a bug. Those bugs can be bacteria, mites, yeast, fungi, fleas, ticks, aka; nasty small blood sucking/chewing/biting parasites. Get to a vet before your pet is bald, bleeding, red, and so itchy that they are miserable.*

- *Anxiety: As a parent, it is our job to provide our kids with a safe household and the building blocks to become successful and acceptable members of society. If your dog barks, lunges, snaps, bites, growls, snarls, harasses, challenges, cowers, urinates in fear, or is unable to deal with normal routine social interactions then your pet needs help. Don't just adjust your life to avoid, mitigate, or excuse the behavior, address it! Understand that you and your actions might be adversely affecting your pet's ability to function appropriately and seek an unbiased, credible third party to help. It is for the sake of you, your pet, and the rest of the members of society. Dog bites, attacks, and even deaths occur because people didn't pay attention to the many warning signs their pet gave them.*

- *Bad breath: Bad breath is always bad teeth (well, not 100% of the time, but often enough). If your pet has bad breath, see your vet. Further, have a dental cleaning that includes thorough probing of all teeth AND have digital dental x-rays taken. Your pet's oral health is intimately tied to their overall health, especially heart disease. If your pet has a murmur take extra efforts to keep the teeth healthy and clean.*

—Dr. Krista Magnifico, DVM, *Diary of a Real-Life Veterinarian*

Introduction

When you are not well, you feel it. When your spouse or another family member doesn't feel well, you hear about it. What if your dog doesn't feel well? You need to see it.

DO YOU KNOW YOUR DOG?

Do you know what is normal for your dog? What if something changed? Would you see it? Would you understand it?

KNOW YOUR DOG

Know your dog's normal vital signs *(pg. 179)*. Know what your dog's body normally feels like. Know your dog's eating and drinking habits, their elimination habits, their activity level, their disposition. Know what their happy face looks like.

I remember the day of Jasmine's neck disaster. There were no signs of trouble the day before or in the morning. She was peacefully resting after her morning potty break as she would have any other day. Nothing crazy went on that you could look back at as the moment when something might have happened.

Around noon she got up ... and just stood there. There was nothing identifiable, nothing I could name or put my finger on. But everything about her looked *wrong*. She stood there, then took a couple of steps backward and stood there some more.

I convinced her to lay back down. I had no idea what I was looking at, but I KNEW *something* was very wrong. I got on the phone with our vet to make sure he could see us later in the day in case things still *weren't right*.

When hubby came home from work, Jasmine did get up to greet him. But by then it was clear that something was indeed *wrong with her, all over the place*. She was stiff, lame on three out of her four legs; her hind end was weak, and she was clearly in a lot of pain. We called the vet to let them know that we were on our way.

We knew that the previously found—but *quiet* anatomical abnormalities—in Jasmine's neck were a ticking bomb. That day the bomb went off.

Don't Shoot the Messenger

When a symptom crops up, understandably, the first instinct is to get all over it and squish it like a bug. *What can I do to make this go away [now]?* I feel the same way. But symptomatic treatments won't get you very far.

A severe enough symptom does need to be tended to because it could kill your dog all by itself, such as severe vomiting or diarrhea. But do not shoot the messenger without hearing out the message.

THE SYMPTOM IS NOT THE REAL ENEMY.

A symptom is a *messenger* telling you about a problem you couldn't otherwise see. If your dog hurt a leg and didn't limp, how would you know the leg was injured?

A symptom is a manifestation of the dog's body dealing with a problem. A dog will limp to prevent further injury and allow the leg to heal.

"Pain is part of the body's defense system, producing a reflexive retraction from the painful stimulus, and tendencies to protect the affected body part while it heals, and avoid that harmful situation in the future. It is an important part of animal life, vital to healthy survival."

~wikipedia

To the dog, the pain is telling them to take it easy. It is telling us to look for the cause.

If your smoke detector goes off, you can just turn it off or smash it, to get rid of the annoying sound. Or if we stick with the metaphor, shoot it!

You could also try venting out the smoke. Which you're going to have to do at some point.

But what about the fire that is the real reason behind it all?

"You wake up in the morning, your water is boiling, your paint is peeling, and your curtains are gone. Which problem do you take care of first? None of them. Your house is on fire!"

~House MD

Not dealing with the real problem allows further damage to occur which could have been prevented.

When you see a symptom, don't shoot the messenger. Go looking for the cause.

Symptom Recognition, Acknowledgment, and Denial

"A symptom is an abnormality caused by a disease that is observable in a sick animal."

~Dictionary of Veterinary Terms:
Vet-speak Deciphered for the Non-veterinarian

The above definition points out two important things. A symptom is an abnormality, and it can be observed.

As far as your dog's health is concerned, this is the most important part of your job. Surely, that's a no-brainer, isn't it? You would be surprised how often it is not.

OBSERVING DOESN'T NECESSARILY MEAN UNDERSTANDING

Sometimes we get so used to certain existing abnormalities, such as fear, that it is very easy to miss their medical significance. If you had a confident dog, who suddenly became fearful, you'd be likely to take notice. But what if your dog is already fearful?

Your dog might be fearful; he might be quiet; he might be reactive. What is most important is knowing what is *abnormal for your dog*.

KNOWING WHAT IS NORMAL

Knowing what is normal requires truly knowing your dog. Nobody else can do this for you.

Some symptoms are hard to miss because they hit you right in the face. Explosive diarrhea, vomiting, bleeding, or severe itchiness … These are easy to notice. Things are not always as obvious, though.

A friend's fearful dog became noticeably more fearful. However, stuff like summertime increase in fears were *normal* for her. What followed was some decrease in activity and stamina; hiding behavior; changes in elimination habits; and hair loss. The little girl had a tapeworm.

If your dog were on chemo, you'd expect some side effects, though, in dogs, those are thankfully, way rarer and less horrible than in people. What if your dog was on chemo and their urine started smelling horribly? It would make sense that it must be from the chemo, right?

Bella was on chemo and started having very smelly urine. She was also drinking and peeing like crazy but that was chalked up the steroids she was on as well. With everything that was happening the symptoms got chalked up to the meds. It all made perfect sense.

A few days later she literally exploded with bloody urine. There was a severe bladder infection, which was in fact behind the smell. Under the circumstances, how would one know what's what?

The best rule of thumb is to discuss any symptom with your veterinarian. Hey, should chemo be doing this? Should we double-check to make sure?

BEWARE OF RATIONALIZATIONS

It is our tendency to nurture denial. A decrease in activity and stamina is easily attributed to weather, being tired from _____ (fill in your rationalization), or *simple* aging. "He just matured and slowed down." There is no such thing, my friend! Dogs don't slow down because they have matured, they slow down because being active has become difficult and/or is accompanied by pain.

Some people consider pain to be *normal* in a senior dog. It shouldn't be.

One time I joined hubby and our guys at a friend's farm. It was just couple days after Jasmine started to favor her front left leg. I was upset about it, and we had an appointment scheduled with her chiropractor.

The friend was complimenting on how great Jasmine was looking and how well she was doing. I agreed but noted I was concerned about her front left leg. "Well, she's eight years old," the friend said.

Yes, she was eight years old. But she was eight ears old three days earlier and was pain free.! Just because a dog gets older it doesn't mean they won a frequent-flyer-pain card!

PAIN IS NOT NORMAL AT ANY AGE

Slowing down, not wanting to jump up on the couch, reluctance to play ... are not signs of maturity, they are symptoms of pain.

Ever since JD was a pup, he would play with his buddy at the farm. They'd play and play all day until they'd drop. But suddenly JD's pal stopped wanting to play with him. What do you think? Had he become too mature for silly play? Or should he be examined for signs of arthritis or other health problem?

THE FROG IN BOILING WATER

Gradual changes are the hardest to notice because they happen a little bit at a time. The insidious changes slowly become the *new normal*. Just like a frog placed in cold water that is slowly heated will not jump out. It never works out so great for the frog.

Any signs that could be attributed to *aging* should be examined.

Using what your dog was like when they were younger can serve as a good baseline. Symptoms of arthritis, Cushing's disease, and other medical issues are all too often attributed to aging.

> *denial n. refusal to admit the truth or reality*

> **~Merriam-Webster**

Nobody wants bad things to happen to their dog. Denial is hoping that what you see isn't what you fear it might be.

The first time Jasmine got up and was limping on her rear left leg, both hubby and I hoped her leg had simply *fallen asleep*. Maybe she just laid wrong. Maybe she was just a little stiff. Hubby, an eternal optimist, God bless his soul, was trying to *sell* one of these explanations to me this day. But experience taught me otherwise. As it turned out, Jasmine was limping because she had busted her knee ligament.

Beware of "maybe it's just" explanations for what you're seeing.

Maybe it's *just the heat* was the first thought of Duncan's parents when he became lethargic and listless. Three days later he collapsed upon arrival to the emergency hospital and was diagnosed with Immune-Mediated Hemolytic Anemia (IMHA).

Our neighbors thought it was *just the heat* when their dog collapsed. He died at the emergency hospital of heart failure. After I sent them there. They would have kept hosing him down, hoping that would do the trick.

And yes, even *just the heat* can be deadly for your dog!

KNOW WHAT IS NORMAL FOR YOUR DOG

Know what is normal for your dog. Note and acknowledge any deviations from it. Noticing and addressing early symptoms can make a world of difference, and in some cases, it can mean the difference between life and death.

Resist denial and rationalizations. I know it's hard. So many times I wanted to ignore something in the hope it didn't exist unless I said it out loud. "If I don't go to the vet with the limp, it's not another busted knee." Well, the knee is either busted or not. Avoidance will not make it go away.

If you find a lump on your dog, you can worry about it, you can ignore, you can wonder if it is serious and you can even dismiss it as unimportant. The "head in the sand" approach will not make scary things disappear. At some point, we all wish that it worked that way, but it doesn't.

The only way to deal with a problem is by facing it. And, if by some chance, you do end up at the veterinarian's office with a false alarm, trust me, it's the better alternative.

"Knowing is always better than not knowing."

~Gregory House, House MD

Where There Is Smoke, There Is Fire

So many times people post questions such as "I think something is wrong with my dog, should I worry?"

Clearly, you are already worried. It is my experience that if you feel that something isn't right with your dog, then something isn't right with your dog. You know your dog better than anybody. Something has grabbed your attention, so it is important. Don't let anybody tell you to shrug it off. Go with your gut.

ONE EXTRA TRIP TO THE VET IS BETTER THAN ONE LESS THAN YOU SHOULD HAVE MADE.

If you're as paranoid as I am, you might make a nuisance of yourself now and then. That is a small price to pay for nipping problems in the bud when something is wrong. It is better to see a vet with *a pimple* than not to see one with a tumor.

Looking back, what I regret is not being paranoid, but letting myself be lulled into false confidence. Why? Because Jasmine paid for it.

NOTHING WRONG?

Ever since she came to us, Jasmine was suffering from digestive issues and bad stools. We kept taking her to vets. They checked stool samples, blood, and never found anything. We were sent home with antibiotics which always temporarily helped. She was put on a prescription diet which, frankly, didn't make any difference.

So what did we do? After a hundred vet visits we accepted what we were told—that her digestive system is *sensitive* and that is the way she is. Meanwhile, we should have kept looking for a vet who would have taken things seriously enough to keep looking for a reason until they found one!

Jasmine was suffering from undiagnosed food allergies which over time developed into eosinophilic gastroenteritis (a type of inflammatory bowel disease, IBD). Her IBD wasn't diagnosed until five years later when we took her to yet another vet for a knee injury consultation!

Nobody mentioned food allergies before and, if they were thinking it, they figured that the prescription diet was supposed to solve it. Except that the food contained the very ingredients Jasmine was allergic to.

Good nutrition is one of the cornerstones of health, and I believe that Jasmine's long-standing digestive issues were at the root of many other problems she ended up having to deal with later on in life.

One bad apple can spoil a whole bunch and one part of your dog's system not working properly will affect the rest of their body.

A friend reached out because her dog kept having a strange chronic cough which kept getting worse. She went to a vet and was told it was nothing. How can something be nothing? It wasn't. I urged her to see a different vet, and she did. According to the new vet, her dog had a dental disease that caused an infection in his mouth, eyes, and throat. That was causing the cough. On top of that, his kidneys were failing which was never mentioned to my friend before, despite the existing blood work results used in the new work-up.!

We all wish our dogs remained healthy for their whole lives and some indeed do. Many, however, will battle health issues at some point or another. Quite often a subtle change is the only clue you might get. Stand your ground and don't stop until you have a clear explanation of what is going on.

HOW CAN YOU TELL YOUR DOG NEEDS A VET'S HELP?

Because our dogs cannot *tell* us what's bothering them, we need to become adept at seeing the signs. Any change in your dog's habits, behavior, and physical appearance should be considered a sign that something is going on. Take note of anything out of the ordinary. Here's a laundry list of things to look for:

- Has your dog suddenly become stubborn?
- Perhaps their hearing isn't working as it used to.
- Has he become withdrawn or snarly?
- Do you think he might be in pain?
- Is he drinking more than he normally does?
- Has his coat changed?
- Have his body proportions changed?
- Does he spend the night pacing around the house?

WHERE THERE IS SMOKE, THERE IS FIRE!

You noticed something. There is a reason for it. Now, get the bottom of it! I've learned the hard way how important this is. Getting a clear diagnosis isn't always easy. Don't settle for 'it's probably nothing' as an answer. How often do you see smoke and there is no fire?

THE HOUSE IS ON FIRE! BRIDGET'S PANCREATITIS

If paying attention to symptoms is important, then getting to the root of the problem is crucial.

Bridget began throwing up in the summer when she was three and half years old. I use the term throwing up lightly—the noises coming from her were the most awful sounds I had ever heard, and I was beside myself when there seemed no end.

After-hours trips were made to the vet, for an injection just to make her quit being sick. The sounds were only part and parcel of the ordeal, which I imagine was just as intolerable to Bridget. So was the reflexive gagging, with mouth drawn back in wrinkles, as well as pacing, licking lips, obsessively licking paws and the floor.

The worst, though, was her behavior of eating anything not nailed down, in an effort to make herself throw up, as dogs do. If allowed, she would have eaten enough grass to kill herself!

I marvel that she is still alive, as she ran out to the garden at the onset of an episode, gobbling down an entire corn cob from the compost and then coming back to the house to throw it up, along with her stomach contents. I ended up having to remove the corn crop with a scythe, chopping it all down, and raking it all up. No more compost. All this was on the hottest day of the summer.

Bridget was treated symptomatically with meds for GI upset, nausea and vomiting many times. These episodes went on all summer long. Most of them happened after clinic hours on weekends or evenings. Or so it seemed. Sitting with her was gut- wrenching. She was a danger to herself, and it was difficult to keep her safe.

Sometimes I had to crate her with nothing at all in the crate. At times she even tried to eat a blanket. The stress was awful. I felt terrible for Bridget and felt helpless. I began to sit bolt upright from a dead sleep thinking I had heard her being sick.

Finally, in the fall of that year, blood work was taken, on a visit to a vet kind enough to take her in, while ours was on vacation.

Her digestive enzymes were out of whack, which along with her other symptoms, was conclusive for pancreatitis.

Bridget has been stable on a low-fat (8 %) and low protein (16 %) diet. I am afraid to experiment with any other diet.

Does Your Vet Listen to You?

There is nothing more frustrating than taking your dog to a vet because of a concern and the vet not taking it seriously. I think it is because people, vets not excluded, come in packing preconceived notions. The best vets you will find, are the ones who can say "I am not sure. I need to think about this." Or maybe they say they want to ask a colleague.

A friend's 5-year-old Mastiff started limping on his hind leg. Perhaps he *tweaked* something. They rested him for a few days, but the limp kept getting worse instead of better. Then they found some weird lumps around his ankle. They took him to a vet. Vet figured it was arthritis and that the lumps were from an unformed dew claw. He gave NSAIDs and recommended to wait for a week and see. No x-rays were taken.

The dog was in more and more pain.

Uncomfortable with the wait-and-see approach, my friend sought a second opinion. After examination, the new vet said that it looked like a torn knee ligament and recommended TPLO (Tibial Plateau Leveling Osteotomy) surgery. They did take x-rays, however, and found a lesion on the bone. It turned out to be bone cancer, osteosarcoma.

We were very fortunate with Jasmine's vet. Not once did he dismiss our concerns or hold back on diagnostic investigations. In the past, though, we had plenty of frustrations with vets not *hearing* us. If you feel your vet is not listening to your concerns, it is time to find one who will.

Something Isn't Right? Work It Out

When I come back from the vet I like to feel reasonably confident, both about the [working] diagnosis and the treatment. This can be easier said than done. Not every diagnosis can be achieved with a stethoscope. The main point is to feel that things are on the right track.

DOES THE DIAGNOSIS MAKE SENSE TO YOU?

Diagnosis is a process. Often it requires further tests and imaging. Most diagnostic tests depend on their interpretation.

Does it all seem to make sense? Did you go to a vet with a limp and come home with a nasal spray?

During the consultation, it is important to keep things on track. Good, two-sided communication is crucial. I do not leave the office until I feel we've got a solid plan and we are on the *same page*.

ARE YOU COOL WITH THE TREATMENT?

However the treatment might sound good on paper, is it going to work for your dog? Will you be willing or able to administer it?

There is no point in taking the meds, leaving the office and then never giving it because you're not comfortable giving that kind of stuff to your dog or you know they won't accept the drops, the pills or spray ...

ONLY AGREE IF YOU ARE GOING TO GO THROUGH WITH IT

On a number of occasions, various vets suggested steroids for Jasmine. They would probably, at least temporarily, make her feel better.

There is a time and place to use them. But in general, for me, steroids are a Hail Mary, last resort medication. I am NOT going to agree to give it unless there is absolutely no other solution. Steroids are excellent anti-inflammatories, a mainstay of treatment for most immune-mediated diseases, and can be useful as part of chemotherapy protocols or a treatment of choice when not going down the full chemotherapy road. But similarly to antibiotics, they are also often used willy-nilly.

The first time ever I agreed to steroids was when Jasmine's neck *went bad*. If there was a time to reach for steroids, that was it. The point here is that I would never walk out of the office with the prednisone in my pocket and the vet thinking I was going to give it if that wasn't going to happen.

WHAT OTHER TREATMENT OPTIONS ARE THERE?

My dog JD happened to get ringworm at the same time Jasmine was recovering from knee surgery. The vet wanted to use a treatment which would require JD wearing *the cone of shame*. JD, with a cone of shame on, in our house, while trying to keep Jasmine's leg safe? Not happening. "We can't do anything that requires a cone of shame for JD," I said. The vet was not impressed, and I could practically hear the swear words going through his mind. But he got over it and came up with a treatment that didn't require JD wearing the cone.

When Cookie was diagnosed with an iliopsoas injury for which the mainstay treatment is strict rest, I voiced the issue immediately. It wasn't going to happen without some serious chemical help. What would be the point of walking out of there with a recommendation for strict rest knowing that it was impossible to follow through with it? Instead, we walked out with a medication to facilitate the recommendation.

TREATMENTS ONLY WORK WHEN THEY ARE ACTUALLY APPLIED

Even the obvious needs mentioning. Some well-meaning pet owners will accept whatever their vet says and take whatever medication they are given yet go home and never do anything. Even the best of treatments only work when applied and applied properly.

Did your dog get antibiotics but they are making him sick? Don't just stop giving it! Talk to your vet. Ask about an injectable alternative, a different antibiotic or a supportive medication to deal with the nausea.

WORKING WITH A HYPOTHESIS

There were enough times when the symptoms I was concerned about could have been from pain. Whether from Jasmine's Inflammatory Bowel Disease (IBD) or some of her musculoskeletal challenges.

We came home with medication that should address that to see whether it would make any difference. That sounded like a reasonable approach to me under the circumstances. So we tried the treatment, but it didn't do anything. It was time to go back to the drawing board. So we did.

WHAT IS THE TREATMENT'S EXPECTED OUTCOME?

Is the treatment actually not working or are you expecting too much too fast?

Along with every medical report, Jasmine's vet always included a disclaimer regarding the treatment, and we were also given a rough timeline of expected response. We were to call back if for any reason we weren't able to follow the recommendations, if we had any questions, or if things weren't going the way they ought to be.

I found the *expected response to treatment timeline* very helpful. It would look something like this:

- Overall a 25 % improvement is expected by Day 2
- 50% by Day 4
- 75% by Day 6
- 100% by Day 10

With more complicated things, such as surgery, the vet's instructions and expected progress were in much greater detail. Day by day, and week by week we could compare the progress with the given information and feel either comfortable or arrange for an interim appointment.

THE DIALOG CONTINUES UNTIL YOUR DOG IS ALL BETTER

Is your dog not accepting the medication? Is it making them worse? Is it making them sick in all new ways? Is your dog not getting any better? Getting worse?

The treatment might not work because the diagnosis or hypothesis is wrong. It might not work because the treatment is wrong. Or it might not work because that particular treatment isn't going to work for your dog.

Go back to the vet. Work it out. And if you're not getting anywhere, seek a second opinion.

The Importance of Second Opinions

You find a small puddle under your kitchen sink and because you're quite sure you didn't spill anything you call a plumber.

The plumber comes and examines it carefully. "It seems to be a minor leak, might stop on its own, why don't you keep an eye on it for a couple of weeks and see what happens," he says.

You pay the plumber and watch it for a couple of weeks, wiping up puddles. If, over the course of another few weeks your plumber kept telling you to get a bigger and bigger container or worse, to turn off the mains so you wouldn't create conditions for your leak, how long would it take before you found yourself another plumber? After the first visit? The second? How long would you put up with this?

With your own dog's health at stake, can you remember a time when you might have let your vet get away with a similar lack of action or thorough investigation?

***

Your dog's health is ultimately in your hands. Recognizing something is wrong is one part of it. Getting to the bottom of the problem is another.

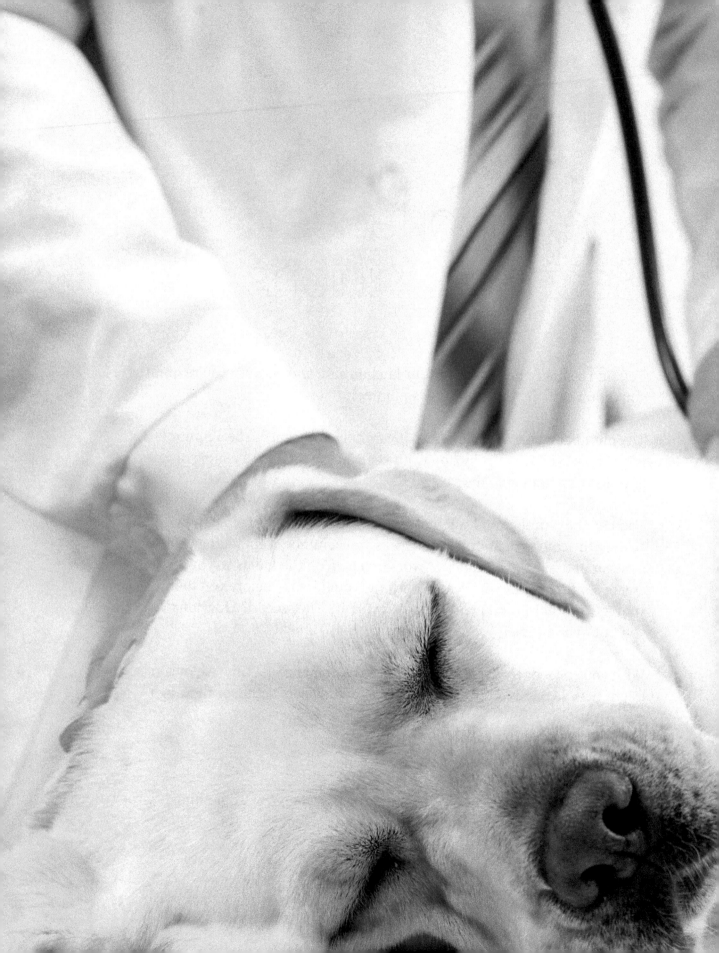

DO I HAVE TO GO TO VET SCHOOL JUST BECAUSE I WANT TO HAVE A DOG?

Of course not. But there are things you had better learn about.

Choosing the right veterinarian and knowing when to seek a second opinion can be the difference between sickness and health, and sometimes the life and death of your dog.

Not all vets were created equal, and even the best vet can make a mistake.

We go to a specialist in veterinary care for their expertise. But sometimes we put our dogs at the mercy of an incompetent vet and worse sometimes that belief in professional care means we question nothing. Or we question things but then do nothing about it. If the situation you find yourself in feels wrong, you have the right to a second opinion!

My brother-in-law's nine-year-old Shepherd started having potty accidents, getting lethargic and having days when she even had difficulty making it out to the yard. They saw a vet, and he diagnosed and started treating her for a Urinary Tract Infection (UTI). The treatment wasn't working, and the dog kept getting worse. Some days she would not move from her bed at all and had to be carried out to potty. Repeat visits to the vet brought no new insights. "Please, see a different vet," we urged. "But we've been seeing this one our whole lives," brother-in-law replied. Eventually, he listened.

The new vet immediately diagnosed hemangiosarcoma, cancer of the spleen. It's a diagnosis with a poor prognosis, but a prompt surgery bought them some quality time together to say good-bye.

A SECOND OPINION DOESN'T ALWAYS GET YOU A DIFFERENT OPINION. BUT IT HAPPENS MORE OFTEN THAN YOU'D THINK.

When we seek a second opinion—whether we don't like the diagnosis or the proposed treatment—what we really want is a *different opinion*. There is nothing wrong with that. Even when the initial diagnosis is confirmed, there is almost always more than one way to treat things. Over time I've learned to gather as many different opinions as I can before making any important medical decisions for my dogs.

When, after she had recovered from her ACL surgeries, Jasmine started limping on her hind leg again, we first took her to the *main* vet. He concluded that she had hurt her muscle.

When her integrative vet examined her, he figured that it was likely a tendon injury.

When we took her to her chiropractor/physical therapist for treatment, she decided that Jasmine had a problem with her knee.

Three vets—three opinions.

In case you're wondering who turned out to be right, it was her *main* vet.

> *"Ten different doctors will come up with ten different diagnoses based on the same data."*
>
> **~Gregory House**

How is it possible that you might get as many different opinions as the number of vets you consult?

Any conclusion is an interpretation of the available facts based on previous experience (or lack of thereof). An expert opinion is made up of information that has been filtered through a human mind so you could say it is inherently subjective.

Though it's really the kind rather than the amount of experience that matters, it will determine where and how the vet will choose to look and how they interpret what they see.

There's truth in the adage: "Choose your specialist - choose your disease." And that applies to everyone.

THE ELEPHANT

It was six men of Indostan
To learning much inclined,
Who went to see the Elephant
(Though all of them were blind),
That each by observation
Might satisfy his mind

The First approached the Elephant,
And happening to fall
Against his broad and sturdy side,
At once began to bawl:
"God bless me! But the Elephant
Is very like a wall!"

The Second, feeling of the tusk,
Cried, "Ho! What have we here
So very round and smooth and sharp?
To me 'tis mighty clear
This wonder of an Elephant
Is very like a spear!"

The Third approached the animal,
And happening to take
The squirming trunk within his hands,
Thus boldly up and spake:
"I see," quoth he, "the Elephant
Is very like a snake!"

The Fourth reached out an eager hand,
And felt about the knee.

"What most this wondrous beast is like
Is mighty plain," quoth he;
" 'Tis clear enough the Elephant
Is very like a tree!"

I'm not going to quote the whole thing. The bottom line is that if you desire a second (or even third, fourth, fifth) *different* opinion, the chances that you will get them are good.

Here comes the catch, though.

NOW THAT YOU HAVE ALL THESE OPINIONS, YOU STILL HAVE TO CHOOSE ONE!

So how do you do that?

One word: Homework.

There is no way around it. Whether it involves finding a vet so awesome that you simply take their word for it, or researching all the possibilities that have been laid out for you, you still do have to do your homework.

You can go with your gut, that often works, but you still need to root it in some information.

Of course, you can always toss a coin. Eeny, meeny, miny, moe …

However you decide to arrive at your decision, make sure you will be able to live with it afterward.

Wellness Exams

Problems can be brewing for quite a while before any visible signs crop up at all. How do you discover a problem before you can see it?

WHY TAKE A DOG TO A VET WHEN THERE IS NOTHING WRONG?

Knowing when to see a vet when your dog is apparently ill is important. But in many cases, when your dog starts showing symptoms, some diseases can already be in their advanced stage.

A regular health evaluation can catch early dental disease, weight issues, orthopedic issues, systemic disease or organ damage. The earlier you discover a problem, the better the prognosis for your dog.

Are any of your dog's organs quietly in trouble? Does your dog have brewing dental disease? Has your dog been infected with Heartworm? You better know these things before they manifest!

A healthy young dog should be seen by a veterinarian at least once a year. Senior dogs should ideally have their checkups at least twice a year.

DO NOT SKIMP ON REGULAR EXAMS

Just don't do it. Just the other day a friend of mine took her dog for a wellness exam. The dog appeared perfectly normal and did not show any signs of a disease. The exam, and subsequent testing discovered a splenic tumor. Whether benign or cancerous, these are typically diagnosed only when the dog crashes, bleeding out internally.

Things can be brewing undetected for a long time before they finally *blow up* on you. By then, you have a major problem.

I admit I don't see a doctor until I think I'm at death's door. But I do take my dogs for wellness exam twice a year, religiously.

When is it an Emergency?

Do you know when you need to drop everything and burn rubber on the way to the emergency?

Too often I see people seeking advice online while they should have been gone to the vet already.

My dog has been vomiting and doesn't pee and has become very weak and is not active anymore. It started off as diarrhea. Please help.

My dog was given a bone to eat. When going for a poo, he was screaming out and whimpering. He passed some but was still straining afterward and screaming out. He's a 4-year-old staff. Any help ideas, please?

My puppy is five months old and is up to date on all her shots. This morning she threw up two socks. She is disoriented and dizzy and can't walk right. Plus she won't eat or drink. What's wrong with my baby?

My Chihuahua got attacked by a pit bull, and she's just laying on the bed and when she breathes her ribs pop out, and she pooped on herself, and there was blood in it what should I do?

My 17-month-old Yorkie has had diarrhea and vomiting badly for three days. He can't hold anything down, even water; he immediately heaves it up. The last 24 hours it has become more frequent and color changed to red at both ends. How serious.

Without exception, all the cases above, of course, are emergencies. The best indication of the seriousness of the situation is your dog's behavior.

When your dog is in high distress, time is wasting. Be on your way to a vet. Knowing when to drop everything and rush to the hospital can be the difference between life and death.

If any of the things listed below happen to your dog, take them to the veterinarian immediately.[1]

Even if your dog seems to be in relatively good shape, all of these conditions are potentially life-threatening, and things could go rapidly downhill. Call the veterinary clinic to let them know you are on your way and to get advice about any first aid that you could provide.

- Any serious trauma (e.g., hit by a car, a fall from a moving vehicle, car accidents, gunshots or deep puncture wounds)
- Electrocution
- Difficulty giving birth
- Animal bites, including snake, strikes by an unknown species
- Burns (chemical or thermal)
- Near drowning
- Smoke or carbon monoxide inhalation
- Apparently broken bones

---

1 http://dawgbusiness.blogspot.ca/2010/09/when-is-it-emergency.html

- Exposure to extremely cold or hot temperatures
- Ingestion of a possible poison (including human and pet medications)

If your dog has any of the following symptoms, talk to a vet immediately, no matter the time of day or night.

- Difficulty breathing
- Severe pain in any part of the body
- Profuse vomiting, particularly associated with an inability to keep down water, blood in the vomit, depression or pain
- Repeated unsuccessful attempts at vomiting, especially if associated with an enlarged abdomen
- Seizures
- A severely depressed attitude or unresponsiveness
- Extreme weakness or wobbliness
- Large amounts of blood in the stool
- Collapse
- Bleeding that drips or pools (a "smear" here and there is probably not an emergency)

It is always safer to make a phone call than to "wait and see." Talking to a veterinarian about your dog's symptoms will help you determine whether or not you need to bring them in immediately or if they can wait until your regular clinic is open for business.

For me, if any of the above were happening, I'd be on my way.

Symptoms to Watch for in Your Dog

Vomiting

Nothing gets a person moving faster than the sound of their dog heaving. If you're lucky, you manage to let your dog out in time. Or you might come home from work to a puddle of vomit by the door.

DOGS ARE BUILT TO VOMIT.

A part of the brain named the "vomiting center" is especially well developed in dogs, and they have a layer of skeletal muscle throughout the length of the esophagus to assist vomiting. This makes good sense given that dogs have the tendency to ingest all kinds of things, some of which have no business in the stomach.

Vomiting is a well-developed protective reflex. It serves to eliminate toxic or irritating substances from the GI tract.

If something doesn't sit right after it's gone down, back out it comes.

Shortly after Cookie wolfed down a whole partridge, she threw up a bunch of feathers. I figured the whole thing was coming back out, but no, the stomach dumped only what it didn't want. Pretty awesome, isn't it?

When JD consumed too much grass and horse poop at the farm, he'd throw it up the next morning. Why he'd eat that again beats me, but at least his stomach is smart enough.

The signs of impending doom might include your dog drooling, licking their lips (or the furniture, the rugs, themselves), swallowing excessively or even funny posture. I can tell when Cookie isn't feeling well even just from her face.

Some dogs seek to eat grass. There is no solid agreement whether that is to encourage vomiting or an attempt to soothe the stomach. Our boys throw up after eating grass, the girls never did.

If my dog vomits just once, looks and acts normally, and I can put my finger on the cause, I don't get overly worried.

The things my dogs have thrown up over time include dead mice, pieces of sticks, rocks, pieces of plastic, a sock (we dodged a bullet with that one), grass, and horse poop mixed with hay …. I am concerned when I find assorted inedible items in the puke, but so far it has always come back out without causing further trouble.

I don't encourage my dogs to eat these things, but I can't watch them every second of every day either.

"Drop it" or "leave it" commands are great if you're at the right place at the right time. But this had even backfired on me when Cookie discovered that grabbing sticks is a great way to acquire treats. She'd drop one and accept her treat only to turn around and grab another one. She thought it was a great game. Eventually, it turned out that ignoring her stick-grabbing behavior was more successful than trying to intervene.

Concerns with inedible items include local issues of damage to the mouth, teeth, and choking. More serious and less obvious problems include gastroenteritis, obstructions, perforations or even toxicity, depending on the item.

Our dogs' taste for inedible things was one of the reasons we took out pet health insurance. Having a lot of free time outside, it is inevitable that the guys ingest something inappropriate from time to time.

DON'T SHRUG IT OFF.

While vomiting is a natural thing it doesn't mean it's always benign. On the contrary, some of the toxins or irritants can do a lot of damage not only by being ingested but also on their way out. Vomiting can also be an indicator of a disease elsewhere in the body.

Note: Sometimes what looks like vomiting is actually regurgitation. While it might look similar, it's a different process *(pg. 87)*.

If a dog keeps vomiting and exhibits signs of distress, it's time to be on your way to the vet.

Signs that you should call your vet include:[2]

- Persistent or severe vomiting
- Projectile vomiting (a sign of possible gastrointestinal obstruction)
- Attempting to vomit but nothing comes out
- Evidence of poison in the vomit (e.g., packaging or bright green dyes that are included in some types of rat poison)
- Vomiting together with other symptoms such as:
  - Loss of appetite
  - Diarrhea
  - Lethargy
  - Weight loss associated with chronic vomiting, inability to keep food down, or lack of interest in the food.
  - Changes in drinking and urinary habits
  - Abdominal pain (hunched posture, unable to get comfortable, pacing, panting, hiding, sensitivity to touch)
  - Abdominal enlargement or distension - especially concerning if happening quickly over an hour
  - Blood in the vomit (partially digested blood looks like coffee grounds; fresh blood is bright red)

---

2   http://www.peteducation.com/article.cfm?c=2+2090&aid=3574

In spite of the *gross factor* involved, examining your dog's vomit might give you important clues as to what's going on.

Dogs do seem to conduct scientific studies on the edibility of almost everything in their environment. However, it's important to remember that their vomiting might have nothing to do with what they recently ate.

While vomiting is often caused by a problem in the GI tract itself, the issue might be originating somewhere else entirely. This is an important distinction to make. Causes of vomiting that have nothing to do with the GI tract itself are typically even more serious.

Problems within the GI tract that cause vomiting include:[3]

- Dietary changes or indiscretions
- Foreign bodies
- Intestinal obstruction
- Food intolerance or sensitivity
- Parasites (roundworms, hookworms, Giardia, coccidia, etc.)
- Viral infections (canine parvovirus, coronavirus, canine distemper, etc.)
- Bacterial infections (Salmonella, E. coli, etc.)
- Bacterial overgrowth
- Intussusception (telescoping of the intestines which causes a functional obstruction)
- Tumors/growths in the GI tract
- Ulcers in the GI tract
- Inflammatory bowel disease

Problems outside the GI tract that can cause vomiting include:[4]

- Pancreatitis
- Kidney disease

---

3   http://www.peteducation.com/article.cfm?c=2+2090&aid=3574
4   http://www.peteducation.com/article.cfm?c=2+2090&aid=3574

- Liver disease
- Hypoadrenocorticism (Addison's)
- Diabetic ketoacidosis
- Toxemia due to infection
- Hypercalcemia (high blood calcium)
- Hyper or hypokalemia (high or low blood potassium)
- CNS disease
- Lead toxicity
- Motion sickness
- Some drugs or medications

If JD or Cookie vomit something inedible, but act normally and are hungry shortly after, I might not even withhold food. I leave it up to them to decide whether they want to eat or not. Our guys are usually good at making the right judgment about that.

If you pay close attention, your dogs will tell you how well or ill they feel.

With her IBD, Jasmine threw up fairly frequently. She'd refuse food; her stomach would make gurgly noises and eventually she'd throw up some bile. After she threw up, she'd usually start feeling better and look for food.

When Cookie had a bout of pancreatitis, she vomited only once, and we were on our way to the vet. Why? Because she was looking sick even before she threw up. She was refusing food and looked tired and lethargic. When she threw up, we hoped that getting it out of her system was going to make her feel better. But because it didn't, we didn't wait any longer.

WHEN IS IT AN EMERGENCY?

- Projectile vomiting, vomiting repeatedly, trying to vomit but nothing coming out, blood (whether fresh or digested) ... mean you need to see a vet ASAP.

- A vomiting dog who is lethargic, weak, shaking or otherwise obviously in distress, needs to see a vet immediately.

- With severe vomiting, your problem isn't only the underlying cause but also the dehydration, acid-base imbalances and electrolyte disturbances caused by the vomiting.

- Waiting too long before seeing a vet could even be fatal.

WHAT'S IN THE VOMIT?

An often overlooked way of determining whether your dog's vomiting is serious is to examine the vomit itself.[5]

Gross factor aside, there really might be some useful information in there. Here's what to look for.

Nothing	As paradoxical as it may sound, a dog that is trying to vomit but nothing is coming up may be in the greatest danger of all. This is a classic symptom of Gastric Dilatation and Volvulus (GDV or bloat), a life-threatening condition that necessitates immediate veterinary attention if an affected dog is to survive.
Bright red blood	If you find any blood in your dog's vomit, call your veterinarian ASAP. It should go without saying that if a dog is bleeding from his gastrointestinal tract, he needs immediate veterinary attention.
Coffee grounds	No, your dog didn't just raid the garbage can, this material is partially digested blood. Call your veterinarian ASAP.
Worms	Yes, dogs can vomit up gastrointestinal parasites. Roundworms are the most likely culprit, particularly in puppies. If your dog has just been dewormed, this is not an immediate cause for concern as long as he is happy, active, eating, drinking, and pooping. Continue with your deworming protocol. If your dog has not been dewormed recently, he needs treatment—call your veterinarian.

---

5   http://dawgbusiness.blogspot.ca/2012/10/whats-in-vomit.html

Frothy yellow or orange-tinged fluid	The froth is mucus mixed with other gastrointestinal fluids. The yellow-orange pigment comes from bile, which is secreted into the upper part of the small intestine. If your dog tends to vomit up fluid like this when his stomach is empty, he may have a condition known as "bilious vomiting syndrome." Most cases can be managed by feeding more frequently throughout the day. Offering two or three small meals rather than one big one will usually do the trick. However, pancreatitis or an intestinal obstruction can also cause your dog to vomit bile on an empty stomach. Always err on the side of caution and see your vet.
Bright green material	Some types of poisons used to kill mice and rats, or snail and slug baits, can be dyed a bright green or blue color. If you notice a green discoloration to your dog's vomit, call your veterinarian immediately.

And while you're poking around in the vomit, collect a sample to bring to your dog's veterinarian should you decide to make an appointment.

The vet may not need it, but if they do you'll be happy you didn't throw it all away.

Diarrhea

Diarrhea is not a disease; it is a symptom of one.

Just as it is with vomiting *(pg. 63)*, dogs can get diarrhea for a straightforward reason, such as *garbage gut* or dietary indiscretion. Acute diarrhea can be self-limiting, meaning it will go away on its own. Chronic diarrhea is always serious.

Diarrhea can signal a serious problem. Focusing on the symptom will not cure the disease. Plus diarrhea too can be caused by problems that have nothing to do with the gut at all.

Focus too much on the diarrhea and you might miss what's really going on. Yes, we all want the diarrhea to stop, but only addressing the cause can do that effectively.

CONSIDER THE BIG PICTURE

- How bad is the diarrhea?
- Is there also vomiting?
- Is the dog lethargic?
- Not interested in food?
- Does the dog look or act sick?

The longer the list of problems, the faster you should be seeking veterinary attention.

Note: *A sick puppy is always an emergency. Don't put your puppy's life at risk by trying to treat them at home without first having them examined by a veterinarian.*

THINK BACK

- Did your dog get into something they shouldn't?
- Eat something unusual or suspicious?
- Did you start a new food or medication?
- Have there been any major changes in your dog's life?
- Even if they have not had access or gotten into anything is it possible they have eaten a tainted piece of food in their own bowl?
- Did you make an abrupt change in your dog's food?
- Did you happen to give your dog food item(s) they are not used to?
- Did your dog get into the garbage?
- Can you recall any stressful events such as holiday visitors, construction in the house, or any changes in your dog's environment or lifestyle? Even excitement or strenuous exercise can result in diarrhea.

Last time JD got diarrhea we definitely had a suspect. While on a walk, he snatched and ate part of an unidentified carcass. Because we did have a suspect and he looked normal otherwise, we decided to try a 24-hour fast followed by bland meals to see whether his gut would settle down. It did.

Acute diarrhea from a dietary indiscretion should start to improve within 24 hours.

On the other hand, one day when Cookie clearly didn't feel well. If she had just one episode of diarrhea, we would have taken her in.

Severe, explosive, unrelenting diarrhea is an emergency.

Stool with blood in it calls for medical attention. Fresh blood from the large intestine is bright red, whereas digested blood appears tarry or black.

If your dog continues to have diarrhea for longer than about 24 hours, you need to see a vet. Do not wait any longer than that.

Just once we waited longer, only to regret it. With her IBD, Jasmine had diarrhea fairly often. She was typically put on Metronidazole, which is an antibiotic but also decreases inflammation in the gut. Every now and then Jasmine's diarrhea would resolve on its own. Hoping that it might do that and trying to avoid yet another course of antibiotics, we decided to wait a second day to see if things were going to improve. By then end of the day she had blood in her diarrhea.

LARGE OR SMALL INTESTINAL DIARRHEA?[6,7,8,9,10]

Knowing the difference between the two can be quite useful.

Large intestinal diarrhea is most commonly caused by primary a GI issue. Small intestinal diarrhea is much more likely to be secondary to another problem such as exocrine pancreatic insufficiency (EPI), Addison's disease and liver disease.

Small intestinal diarrhea tends to be the worse and more dangerous of the two. The main jobs of the small intestine are digestion and nutrient and fluid absorption. When it's not working properly, it not only results in diarrhea, but dogs may also not be getting the nutrition they need.

---

6   http://dawgbusiness.blogspot.ca/2010/10/tale-of-many-tailsand-what-came-out.html
7   http://dawgbusiness.blogspot.ca/2010/10/stories-from-my-diary-rrhea-part-ii.html
8   http://dawgbusiness.blogspot.ca/2010/11/stories-from-my-diary-rrhea-part-iii.html
9   http://dawgbusiness.blogspot.ca/2010/11/stories-from-my-diary-rrhea-part-iv.html
10 http://dawgbusiness.blogspot.ca/2010/11/stories-from-my-diary-rrhea-part-v.html

Common causes of small intestinal diarrhea can be quite scary, including parvovirus. Many of the other possibilities aren't a whole lot better. I would not take my chances with small intestinal diarrhea.

With small intestinal diarrhea, your dog might not have to go more than two to four times a day, but they will produce huge amounts of very wet stool. If there is blood in the stool, it is dark, digested blood and can resemble coffee grounds. With ongoing small intestinal diarrhea, your dog can start losing weight.

A dog with acute large intestinal diarrhea will need to go frequently, usually in a hurry. He is likely to strain while defecating and pass only small amounts at a time. There can be fresh blood or mucus in the stool. If there is no fresh blood, mucus, straining, or small amounts frequently, your dog has small intestinal diarrhea.

There is no loss of nutrients with large intestinal diarrhea and weight loss is unlikely.

Large intestinal diarrhea can be caused by parasites, inflammatory bowel disease, stress-induced colitis, cancer, bacteria, fungal infections, garbage gut and other dietary issues.

When dogs have conditions that affect both the large and small intestine, a combination of symptoms can be seen.

DON'T MAKE THIS BIG MISTAKE

The biggest mistake you can make is to think that your dog is constipated because they are straining or posturing to defecate while in fact, they are straining with watery diarrhea. Trying to treat it with laxatives will only make things worse. Never assume your dog is constipated unless they have a history of this, or are diagnosed by your vet.

SOME TIPS FOR DIFFERENTIATING BETWEEN THE TWO TYPES OF DIARRHEA.

Characteristics of small intestinal diarrhea
- large volumes infrequently
- watery
- may be projectile
- if blood is present, it's usually digested (melena)
- no straining (tenesmus)
- may be yellow-green in color
- if chronic, often associated with weight loss
- may be associated with vomiting
- may be associated with flatulence
- appetite may be reduced

Characteristics of large intestinal diarrhea
- small amounts frequently
- straining often present
- the presence of bright red blood or mucus
- appetite usually unaffected
- if associated with vomiting it is usually infrequent and unrelated to eating
- usually no weight loss

WHEN TO TAKE A DOG TO THE VET?

Diarrhea is such a common problem that most people want to treat it on their own. After all, we don't see the doctor every time we get diarrhea. Many home remedies, such as a 24-hour fast, bland food, and adding fiber or probiotics to the diet can be helpful. But trying to treat diarrhea without understanding the cause behind it is often counterproductive and can be dangerous.

THE FIRST STEP IS FIGURING OUT WHAT CAUSED IT

Diarrhea can be caused by any of the following things (and more!):[11]

- Dietary indiscretion
- Diet change
- Foreign body/obstruction
- Intestinal parasites
- Stress
- Food allergy or intolerance
- Bacterial infections
- Viral infections
- Fungal infections
- Toxins
- Pancreatic disease
- Auto-immune disease
- Liver disease
- Kidney disease
- Cancer
- Addison's disease

Do you still feel confident that you can always deal with your dog's diarrhea on your own?

---

11 http://www.peteducation.com/article.cfm?c=2+2090&aid=3553

WHEN IS IT AN EMERGENCY?

- if diarrhea lasts longer than 24 hours despite symptomatic treatment (24 hour fast followed by small frequent meals of bland, low-residue diet)

- if there are any signs of dehydration (skin tent, sticky gums)

- if there is any associated lethargy, vomiting or other symptoms (i.e. it's not 'just' diarrhoea)

- if there is blood in the stool

WHAT'S IN THE POOP?

APPEARANCE

Nobody wants to spend too much time with their dog's poop, particularly when it's bad. But examining it can give you useful information.

Our guys get a bad poop now and then. This is more a reflection of what they got into than an actual health issue. If the stools are consistently or chronically abnormal, though, I am motivated to figure out what's behind it.

WHAT'S IN THE CONSISTENCY?

To some degree, consistency can depend on the dog and their diet. However, stool shouldn't be consistently too hard or too loose.

Diarrhea is a more common problem than constipation. In fact, people often think that their dog is constipated when in fact the dog is actually experiencing diarrhea. See the last chapter where I talk about the difference between small and large intestinal conditions. Lots of straining with nothing coming out can be a sign of large bowel diarrhea as well as constipation. It is important not to try to treat constipation without having a *solid* confirmation (pun intended).

Constipation may be caused by insufficient fiber and water intake but can also have a more serious underlying cause.

Because of Jasmine's inflammatory bowel disease, I kept a detailed chart where I entered day-to-day information, including her stool quality and a number of bowel movements.

There are various fecal scoring charts out there, going into various amount of detail. Here is a quick reference table:

Nothing	Lots of straining and hunching that doesn't produce any poop at all. Your dog could be constipated or have an obstruction. Severe diarrhea and colitis can cause similar symptoms *(pg. 72)*. In either case, see a vet.
Small, dry, hard pellets	Constipation. A couple of times Cookie produced hard stools from eating too many bones and not enough vegetables. Things went back to normal with a correction in her diet. Constipation can have serious causes and effects. If Cookie had hard poops for more than one or two bowel movements and it didn't resolve with adjusting her food, I would take her to the vet.
Firm but not hard, dry logs that look segmented	That's good poop in my books. With Jasmine, every time she had a poop like that was cause for celebration.
Moist and soggy but still formed	This kind of poop puts me in an alert mode. But JD and Cookie get these every now and then with the next poop being normal again. Something didn't sit right, but the body sorted it out. When Jasmine got these, it meant her IBD was starting to act up. A dog who has this type of stools consistently needs to see a vet.

 **Pudding; poop that loses form once it hits the ground. Some texture but no shape.**	This gut isn't happy. When it continues for more than one or two bowel movements, it's time to do something. Could mean intestinal parasites, such as Giardia, intestinal infections (bacterial, viral or fungal), immune/inflammatory disorders, metabolic diseases (e.g., liver failure), heart disease, cancer, and more.
 **Watery**	The gut is really unhappy. When Jasmine got these, her gut was in trouble. Large volumes of watery diarrhea, with or without blood in it, can be an emergency, particularly in smaller dogs and puppies.

WHAT'S IN THE COLOR?

Healthy poop is typically brown.

What makes poop brown is bile, a fluid released from the gallbladder that aids in the digestion and absorption of fats and fat-soluble vitamins and helps eliminate certain waste products from the body.

There can be some variation in color depending on what your dog ate, particularly when you're feeding a variety of foods. Some manufactured diets will make dogs produce what might otherwise be considered abnormal stool (like the extremely light feces that are formed when dogs eat a prescription, soy-based, hydrolyzed diet) but if your dog is consistently on one type of food, you'll get a feel for what's normal for them.

Unless your dog just ate a box of crayons (as happened with Roxy), poop that is any color other than shades of brown is often a red flag that something is wrong.

Changes in color usually go hand in hand with changes in consistency.

For example, Exocrine Pancreatic Insufficiency (EPI) may result in clay-colored diarrhea, caused by the pancreas being unable to produce the enzymes needed to digest food and inflammation, and swelling blocking the passage of bile. Pale stools can indicate a lack of bile production or flow, suggesting liver and/or gallbladder disease.

Brown	Brown poop is happy poop.
Orange	The dog's biliary system is blocked, or his or her blood cells are rupturing within the circulatory system.
Pale or clay-colored	Also called acholia, pale or clay-colored stools can develop as a result of gallbladder, liver, or pancreatic disease.
Yellow or greenish	Yellow or greenish stools are sometimes produced when material is passing through the intestinal tract more quickly than normal. It can be seen with Giardia, intestinal parasites or infections, and many other conditions.
Black, tarry	When your dog's stool looks like this, it signifies bleeding in the upper digestive tract or respiratory tract (with the blood being coughed up and swallowed). The black, tarry appearance is due to the presence of digested blood. Potential causes range from GI ulcers, trauma, foreign bodies, infections, tumors, blood clotting disorders, kidney failure and more.

Bright red streaks/bloody	This indicates bleeding in the lower GI tract. Lower GI tract bleeding can be caused by colitis (inflammation or infection of the colon/large intestine) or conditions affecting the anus or anal glands. Jasmine sometimes got blood in her stool when her IBD was acting up. Enteritis and colitis can be caused by IBD, intestinal parasites, infections, foreign bodies, stress, and more. Hemorrhagic Gastro-Enteritis (HGE) is a common cause of blood-stained diarrhea in dogs. This is a serious condition that can occur very quickly and be fatal if left untreated. Bloody diarrhea in puppies could mean the dreaded Parvovirus, particularly if your pup is also vomiting and lethargic. In older dogs, it could be a sign of cancer.
Bright green	Bright green stools can be caused by your dog ingesting certain types of rat poison or snail bait. This means an immediate trip to a vet.
Polka dot stool	If you find rice-like specks or spaghetti-like strands, you're probably looking at worms.

WHAT'S IN THE COATING?

Healthy poop should not have any coating on it.

Sometimes you'll find stool that is covered by a slimy substance - mucus. Mucus is produced in the intestine to lubricate and protect the gut lining, but normally it isn't noticeable on feces.

Mucosal surfaces in the gut are part of the immune system, designed to detect and kill pathogenic organisms that may be trying to make their way through the gut lining.

When the large intestine isn't happy and battling parasites, bacterial overgrowth, food allergy or intolerance, or even tumors (basically anything that irritates or inflames the gut wall), it can result in an increased production of mucus, which then becomes apparent on the stool. Even stress can cause mucus-coated stools.

One or two slimy stools don't warrant rushing to a vet.

However, if this becomes a regular occurrence, or it is combined with other symptoms such as diarrhea, vomiting or abdominal pain, the situation in the gut has gotten out of control, and it's important to have your dog seen by a vet.

WHAT'S IN THE CONTENT?

Just like with vomit, the contents of your dog stools can sometimes provide an inkling as to what may have upset your dog's digestive system.

Pieces of plastic, toys, and other non-food items can be an obvious cause for bad stools. One question left unanswered, however, is whether all the foreign material has passed or some still remains within the digestive tract.

If you find bits of undigested food, it's either a reflection of the food or of your dog's ability to digest what they eat.

Things like pieces of raw carrots can appear in the stools in more or less pristine shape. Dogs are not designed to digest chunks of raw vegetables. Once I tried giving my dogs a freeze dried raw food with chickpeas in it. Chickpeas are nutritious and seemed like a good ingredient. However, the chickpea grit came out unchanged. Clearly, there was little to no nutritional benefit to that.

If food that dogs should normally digest well comes out untouched, then you have a serious problem on your hands.

If your dog's stools look greasy, you might be looking at a condition that prevents the intestinal tract from absorbing nutrients (malabsorption).

ONE BAD POOP, NO BAD POOP

Bad poops happen, particularly since dogs tend to eat all kinds of things, some of which are not meant to be eaten. If my dogs get a bad poop, I watch for other signs of a problem such as changes in appetite, drinking, vomiting, lethargy or anything else that seems off. If the dogs look fine and the next poop is the way it should be, I just file the event in the back of my mind (and in Cookie's case on her chart).

If it develops into diarrhea, I generally give it 24 hours to resolve. If it doesn't, or if it becomes severe, or accompanied by other signs mentioned above, I see a vet.

There are a number of things that affect stool quality and diet is definitely one of them. In an otherwise healthy dog, it can even be as simple as determining the right amount of dietary fiber for that individual. It be quite a balancing act, particularly in large breed dogs. But before you make any assumptions and start playing with your dog's diet, see a vet to make sure you know what you're dealing with.

DON'T FORGET THE SAMPLE

Your vet can get a lot more information from your dog's poop than you ever could. Not only do they evaluate all the above aspects, but they can also further analyze it and take a detailed look at what's in the poop that is hidden from view by performing a microscopic fecal analysis.

If you have any concerns, bring a poop sample with you.

Regurgitation

REGURGITATION IS NOT VOMITING[12]

What is the difference between the two and does it matter?

Vomiting *(pg. 63)* is the forceful expulsion of stomach contents. A dog will be nauseous—they might drool or lick their lips right before they throw up. You will typically see dogs heaving as they vomit because vomiting always involves abdominal effort.

Regurgitation is a more passive process that involves the expulsion of the contents of the esophagus. In other words, it just blobs out.

No heaving is involved.

Jasmine vomited plenty of times but regurgitated only once or twice. There was a distinct difference. When she regurgitated, it was almost immediately after she finished her meal and it came out the same as it went down (well, in kind of a sausage shape). She just opened her mouth, and there it came.

When she vomited, it was always preceded and accompanied by heaving sound, followed by my mad dash to open the door to let her out. She always tried to take it outside, so it was up to me whether or not I made it there on time.

---

12 http://www.veterinarypartner.com/Content.plx?A=2809

Both Jasmine and Cookie sometimes had what I call "wet burps" where some stomach juices with or without bits of food just spilled out. Again, there was no heaving.

If you see bile (a yellowish-brown tinged fluid) it means that you're looking at vomit.

But not all vomit contains bile. Every now and then JD would overdo it at the farm munching on horse poop and grass. What he would vomit the next morning looked almost like poop. You could clearly see what he feasted on the previous day, and there was no bile in it at all. There was a lot of heaving, though.

WHY WOULD A DOG REGURGITATE?[13,14]

The most common causes of regurgitation are partial or complete obstruction of the esophagus or an esophageal motility issue. It means that the food (or liquid) is unable to make its way to the stomach and builds up in the esophagus instead.

An obstruction can be caused by a foreign body, stricture (narrowing), vascular abnormality (blood vessels that form a tight ring around the esophagus) or a tumor.

Problems with motility can be caused by inflammation, Addison's disease, neuromuscular disorder or toxins. Megaesophagus—a disorder with several, potential underlying causes—is a common cause of regurgitation in dogs.

Frequent regurgitation puts your dog at risk of developing aspiration pneumonia, which happens when food is accidentally inhaled into the lungs.

---

13 http://www.petmd.com/dog/conditions/digestive/c_multi_regurgitation
14 http://www.petplace.com/article/dogs/diseases-conditions-of-dogs/symptoms/regurgitation-in-dogs

Regurgitation can also be one of the symptoms of Gastroesophageal Reflux (GERD).[15]

This is kind of a reversed process to the above. Rather than food or liquid being unable to make its way down, fluids from the stomach make their way up into the esophagus.

Causes include things such as Inflammatory Bowel Disease (IBD), chronic pancreatitis, infections, parasites, liver problems ... pretty much anything that causes prolonged vomiting... as well as hiatal hernias (movement of abdominal contents through the diaphragm around the esophagus), or anesthetic procedures during which dogs are positioned on their backs for long periods of time.

As you see, causes of regurgitation are quite different from those behind vomiting. Treatment then will be very different also. As always, proper diagnosis is the starting point.

Understanding the difference can help you in explaining to your vet what is going on. Or, when in doubt, just bring a sample of whatever came out of your dog.

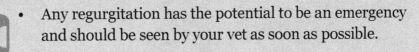

WHEN IS IT AN EMERGENCY?

- Any regurgitation has the potential to be an emergency and should be seen by your vet as soon as possible.

15 http://www.petmd.com/dog/conditions/digestive/c_multi_gastroesophageal_reflux

Panting

Dogs pant. They pant when they exercise, when they are hot, they pant when they are excited. Dogs pant, and it is perfectly normal. Most of the time.

WHEN TO WORRY ABOUT PANTING

Jasmine started with panting and pacing episodes when she was about two and a half years old. Usually in the middle of the night. She'd get restless, wander around and pant, without a discernible reason. She was clearly unhappy. Something was wrong.

In order to be able to tell when to worry you need to know your dog, you need to know what is normal for them. Excessive or unexplained panting can be a symptom of a serious problem.

When our guys come from a good romp outside, or it is hot, or something exciting is happening, I expect them to pant. I'd be concerned if they didn't.

If they continue to pant by the time they should have calmed or cooled down, I start paying attention.

OBESITY[16]

The most common cause of excessive panting in dogs is obesity. An obese dog is more likely to overheat, and activity is more exhausting for them. This is comparable to an overweight person climbing a flight of stairs huffing and puffing and becoming red in the face.

If your dog is so overweight that they pant heavily with very little exercise, you have a serious problem. Obesity shortens life span and spawns all kinds of health problems including heart disease, pancreatitis, joint disease, liver disease ... and even cancer.[17]

Not to mention that quality of life goes down the drain. I still remember Jasmine's old friend who became so overweight and miserable; he no longer enjoyed anything other than more food.

HEATSTROKE[18]

The hotter your dog gets, the more they'll pant. Make no mistake, though; panting cannot always cool your dog off sufficiently in hot conditions, particularly paired with exercise. Heatstroke can cause catastrophic damage to your dog's body and can lead to brain damage and even death.

If your dog is panting heavily and you have a reason to suspect heatstroke, check for other signs. If your dog's gums and tongue are deep red, purple or blue with thick, sticky saliva, move your dog to a cool place and spray them with cool (not cold) water or place wet rags or towels over them, particularly near the stomach and inside of legs. Do not immerse your dog in cold water! If your dog's temperature reaches 104 degrees Fahrenheit (40°C) take your dog to a vet immediately (preferably with cool rags applied).

---

16 http://www.petmd.com/blogs/fullyvetted/2012/jan/panting_normal_or_not-12320
17 http://www.peteducation.com/article.cfm?c=2+1659&aid=694
18

Note: Other signs of heat stroke include vomiting and diarrhea. Dogs suffering from severe heatstroke are actually likely to stop panting.

FEVER

A heatstroke is hyperthermia due to environmental causes. Fever is triggered by your dog's immune system. Your dog might get a fever as a response to infection or other illness. Fever can be accompanied by loss of appetite, lethargy, changes in behavior and other signs. If your dog has a fever, see a veterinarian to determine the underlying cause. As with heatstroke, temperature over 104 degrees Fahrenheit is an emergency and needs immediate medical attention.

When Jasmine developed severe drug-induced hyperthermia, she almost died. She spent a week in a hospital, and it took her a month to recover. She couldn't walk; she was peeing brown urine ... she was in horrible shape. Ever since I've been paranoid about body temperature increase in my dogs. I take care to monitor changes in the color of the gums and tongue, armed with a thermometer and checking the temperature when in doubt.

PAIN

Panting can be a response to pain. Any stress, psychological or physiological, can result in panting.

When Jasmine started her episodes of panting and pacing, pain was the number one suspect. While we were trying to find the reason for what was happening, there were many possible causes on the table to consider, investigate, and rule out, just to make their way back on the drawing table. With everything said and done, I think it was pain from her problematic neck after all.

If your dog is panting and salivating excessively, retching and has distended abdomen, he might be suffering from bloat. Bloat is a life-threatening condition, take your dog to a vet immediately!

Don't forget to consider pain as a reason for your dog's unexplained panting.

RESPIRATORY OR CARDIOVASCULAR DISORDERS

It figures that respiratory and cardiovascular disorders can cause excessive panting in your dog. Jasmine's heart and lungs were checked a number of times when we were trying to get her episodes diagnosed.

HORMONAL IMBALANCES

Excessive panting can also be a sign of hormonal disorders, such as hypothyroidism or Cushing's disease. Panting could be accompanied by other symptoms, such as weight gain, excessive drinking, coat changes, changes in appetite or behavioral changes.

BOTTOM LINE

These are just some of the causes of excessive panting in dogs. If your dog is panting excessively, or without an obvious reason, take it seriously and consult your veterinarian. I know I say this all the time. But that's the point— you need to know when to take your dog to the vet.

WHEN IS IT AN EMERGENCY?

- the dog is distressed
- the dog has been exposed to high ambient temperatures and is showing any other signs such as weakness or tremors.
- panting associated with lethargy
- unexpected panting with no obvious cause

Drooling

Dogs drool! Some will drool more, some less, depending on the breed and other factors. It is our observation that girl dogs drool less if at all. All our past and present boy dogs have drooled a lot. JD's waterworks could turn a desert into a lush garden.

SALIVA IS A GOOD THING

Not necessarily all over your Sunday outfit, but it serves an important function in your dog's mouth. It is an enzyme-rich liquid that lubricates food and starts the digestive process. That's why most of the waterworks get turned on in anticipation of a meal.

WHAT CONSTITUTES EXCESSIVE DROOLING?

Excessive doesn't mean more than you'd like, but more than would be normal for your dog, whatever that may be. This is always the key.

EXCESSIVE DROOLING IS TYPICALLY ASSOCIATED WITH A PROBLEM IN THE MOUTH, STOMACH, OR ANYWHERE IN BETWEEN

Some of the reasons your dog might start drooling excessively include foreign objects or injuries to the mouth, dental issues, tumors in the mouth, ingestion of irritating or caustic substances or stomach upset.

If your dog starts drooling when there is no food around, it's a good time to check for anything that might be stuck in the gums, tongue, roof of the mouth or between the teeth. While at it, look for bleeding, wounds, ulcers, and other deviations from normal appearance.

With ingestion of a caustic material, red or discolored oral tissues and pain are typical. Some possible culprits include frogs, bugs, toxins, chemicals and household cleaners. Our guys have no access to chemicals or cleaners, but there are toads and bugs around. The toads around here are not severely toxic but getting her mouth on a toad can make Cookie drool and foam quite a lot. Jasmine would also drool like crazy when she accidentally tasted some of her pain medications.

Periodontal disease, tooth root abscesses, fractured teeth, and oral infections or inflammation can all lead to excessive drooling and also a lot of pain. When I suspect any of these things, I see a vet right away.

We also look for any lumps, bumps or any tissue that looks strange. Oral cancer is serious business.

While foreign objects and injuries might be a judgment call, always see your veterinarian if you suspect dental disease or find any strange masses or pigmentation in your dog's mouth.

WHEN IT'S NOT THE MOUTH

If you didn't find any problem in the mouth, you might not be out of the woods.

Excessive drooling might be a result of a problem not related to the mouth. Jasmine (I know I said that girl dogs don't drool) drooled when her stomach was upset. Nausea causes drooling. So can neurological diseases that impair a dog's ability to swallow.

Excessive drooling can be one of the signs of heat stroke, though in such cases you're likely to get tipped off by excessive panting first. Do get familiar with the early symptoms of heat stroke; it is a life-threatening situation.

Pain or anxiety of any origin can result in excessive drooling. Drooling often occurs before vomiting and seizures.

PAY ATTENTION

Know what is normal. Don't dismiss anything out of the ordinary. Symptoms usually like company, so look for other signs, such as bad breath, fever, changes in appetite, changes in behavior ... Always listen to your dog.

WHEN IS IT AN EMERGENCY?

- Warning signs of a potential emergency include pain, an inability to swallow, difficulty breathing, vomiting, lethargy, a foul odor from the mouth, weakness, extreme agitation, or any profuse drooling.

- If you have the least suspicion that your dog ingested a toxic chemical or a cleaner, see a vet immediately.

- A change in mentation, or attitude is cause for grave concern and your dog should see the vet immediately.

- Dogs suffering from gastric dilatation and volvulus (GDV) also tend to drool a lot because the entrance to the stomach is twisted shut. If your dog is drooling, trying to vomit but little or nothing comes up, has a distended abdomen, and is in pain, get him to the veterinarian IMMEDIATELY. Most dogs appear to have a distended abdomen and appear bloated. This is an emergency where seconds count. DO NOT WAIT!

Changes in Gum Color

BECOME FAMILIAR WITH THE NORMAL APPEARANCE OF YOUR DOG'S GUMS AND TONGUE

If you see your dog's gums are red and swollen, you're looking at gingivitis (inflammation of the gums). Where there is gingivitis, there is pain and likely further dental problems below the surface. Gingivitis leads to periodontitis, which in the simplest of terms is characterized by bleeding gums and loss of bony support for the teeth. Oral problems that involve infection always involve bad breath.

Any new lumps, bumps, growths or local discolorations, particularly darkly pigmented areas, of the mouth, tongue and gums should also be examined by your veterinarian.

HYPERTHERMIA/HEATSTROKE

During hot summer months, I pay close attention to the color of my dogs' tongue and gums.

As soon as my dogs' tongue and gums start getting deeper pink in color, it is a signal to me that it is time to take a break and cool-down. I am very paranoid about this and watch closely to register even subtle changes.

As the dog's body gets hotter, the color gets progressively darker. Eventually, it may turn brick red or even purple or blue (as oxygen saturation declines). These are signs of an emergency, and you don't want to let things get that far.

Another sign that your dog is getting too hot is increased panting. I noticed that even with seemingly typical panting (as in play) when my guys are getting hotter, their tongues will stick out further and become wider than usually. Time for a break and cool-down.

Tongues that are even a couple of shades darker than normal beg for action.

Don't ever underestimate the damage heat stroke can cause to your dog's body. There is a point of no-return (from where it is impossible to recover).

OTHER SERIOUS CONDITIONS THAT CAN CAUSE YOUR DOG'S MUCOUS MEMBRANES CHANGE FROM THEIR NORMAL APPEARANCE

Mucous membranes that are bright red, pale, white, yellow, orange, blue or purple indicate a serious medical problem which requires immediate veterinary attention.

Bright red	Besides heat stroke, bright red color might indicate fever, severe infection, poisoning, smoke inhalation, or abnormal levels of red blood cells, which can be caused by dehydration, chronically low blood oxygen levels or bone marrow disease.
Blue or purple	Blue or purple membranes indicate a lack of oxygen, which can be caused by heart disease, poisonings, or respiratory problems.
Yellow or orange	Yellow or orange membranes (i.e., jaundice) are typically associated with liver disease/jaundice or red blood cell disorders.

Pale, gray or white	Pale, gray or white membranes can be a sign of anemia, shock, blood loss, severe dehydration, and more.
Red splotches	Gums with red splotches may indicate a blood clotting problem.

OTHER THINGS TO CHECK

Other things you can check by examining your dog's gums are capillary refill time and level of dehydration/hydration status.

Dry, sticky gums are a sign of dehydration. This is particularly important when your dog is suffering from vomiting or diarrhea or has stopped eating or drinking.

Slow capillary refill time is another sign of a critical illness. To check this, press a finger firmly on the dog's gums for about three seconds. The area you pressed on will be paler than the surrounding tissue. The color should return to normal in about one and a half seconds. If it takes longer than that, it could be a sign of low blood pressure or poor circulation (e.g., from heart disease or dehydration), another indication that your dog is very sick.

WHEN IS IT AN EMERGENCY?

- Most of the above changes in appearance in your dog's gums and tongue are likely to be accompanied by other serious signs and I would consider them all an emergency.

Excessive Drinking

Even though we hardly ever think of it that way, water is the number one essential nutrient. Without water, there is no life. Every function in the body requires water.

How much water does your dog need depends on a number of factors including their size, diet, activity level, and environmental temperature. Hot weather and exercise will naturally make your dog drink more. But if your dog starts acting as if they're trying to drown themselves, something is amiss.

I was talking to a friend about post-op issues her dog was having after knee surgery. She mentioned that in the snow they noticed that her dog's urine was clear (no color at all) and she asked whether it was something to worry about.

I asked if her dog was drinking a lot. Her dog had been unusually thirsty and drinking large amounts of water ever since her surgery three months prior.

I sent them to their vet. The problem was with the dog's kidneys. Unfortunately, just because you're dealing with one problem, it doesn't mean there cannot be another.

EXCESSIVE DRINKING SHOULD BE TAKEN SERIOUSLY

Never withhold or limit water. If you think your dog is peeing too much and offering less water will help, you are putting their health at risk. They are drinking because their body tells them they need to.

WHAT CONSTITUTES EXCESSIVE DRINKING?

There is a calculation you could do to find out how much water your dog should be drinking. The amount they need to drink depends on other things, though, such as the type of food they get. My rule of thumb is that when I start wondering why my dog is suddenly drinking so much, I look for a cause. I think we can be quite tuned into noticing changes, particularly when they happen over a short period of time.

If you want some precision to the observation, you can measure the water that you pour for your dog over a few days and work out how much on average they are drinking per day. Anything greater than 100 ml/kg/day is excessive. Of course, this gets a bit trickier if you have multiple dogs in the house as we do.

SOMETIMES DRINKING MORE MAKES SENSE

When the weather gets warmer, dogs will naturally drink more to replenish the water lost with panting. Same applies to exercise. When Cookie comes from her romp, she's always thirsty. With any fresh snowfall, both our guys will eat as much of it as they can fit. I don't think that even has anything to do with thirst. I suspect it's like ice cream to them and they enjoy the experience. Paying attention to circumstances is necessary.

PAY ATTENTION

Note any change in your dog's drinking or eating habits. Don't dismiss drinking more than usual without an obvious explanation—such as hot weather or exercise. Do you have to fill the water bowl more often lately? Does your dog urinate more frequently? Does the urine lack color? Talk to your veterinarian.

Depending on other symptoms, excessive drinking can be a sign of a number of serious, life-threatening conditions, including:[19]

- Diabetes mellitus
- Cushing's Syndrome
- Addison's disease
- Liver or kidney disease
- Uterine infection
- Hyperthermia
- Poor diet
- and other serious conditions

Certain drugs, such as steroids, can also make your dog more thirsty and hungry than normally. When Jasmine was on steroids for her neck injury, her thirst seemed unquenchable.

A friend's dog started drinking like there was no tomorrow. She couldn't get enough. Always thirsty. They tried withholding water, but the dog was going out of her mind. It turned out she had Cushing's.

WHEN IN DOUBT, ERR ON THE SIDE OF CAUTION

See your vet and bring a urine sample, preferably from the first morning's evacuation. It must be fresh (less than 6 hours) and refrigerated if stored. Untreated problems only get worse and can cause further damage.

19 http://www.petmd.com/dog/conditions/urinary/c_multi_polydipsia_polyuria

WHEN IS IT AN EMERGENCY?

Excessive thirst is usually not an emergency except in situations such as

- guzzling loads of water and vomiting it back up (vomiting is the more concerning symptom here though)

- excessive thirst is sometimes the most obvious symptom in an intact female with pyometra - infection in the uterus. This is a life-threatening condition and must be seen immediately.

Changes in Urination/Urinary Accidents

Dogs don't pee in the house because they are absentminded (unless they have cognitive dysfunction syndrome), don't care, or are trying to get back at you for leaving them alone, losing their favorite toy or not giving more treats. Dogs don't like soiling their dens, and they don't do it out of spite.

DON'T PUNISH YOUR DOG FOR URINATING INDOORS

Urinary accidents in housetrained dogs are signs of medical or behavioral problems. In either case, punishment is the last thing they need.

A house trained dog will pee in the house for one of the following reasons:

- They could not hold it any longer
- They didn't realize it was happening
- They are scared
- They are trying to appease you (submissive urination)

Submissive urination is not a health issue, but I felt I should include it here because it is important to recognize it for what it is. Punishing it will only make matters worse.

ALWAYS LOOK FOR A PHYSIOLOGICAL REASON FIRST

Is your dog drinking more than usual? Peeing while rushing to the door? Peeing while sleeping? Peeing inside the house while straining or producing just a few dribbles when outside?

Naturally, increased drinking and increased urination go hand in hand. But why is that happening? Is your dog's body contending with an infection, excess sugar, excess hormones, toxic substance ...?

Potential causes include:

- Diabetes mellitus
- Cushing's disease
- Addison's disease
- Liver or kidney disease
- Urinary tract infections (UTI)
- Some medications, such as steroids or, of course, diuretics
- Congenital abnormalities
- Neurological issues, and
- Spinal cord injuries or degeneration

Obesity is a common risk factor. Spayed female dogs can develop urinary incontinence associated with low estrogen levels, which leads to weakening of the sphincter muscle.

Shortly after our guys gorge on fresh snow, their bladders are ready to explode.

And, yes, if incontinent Cookie is going to leak, she is most likely to do so on the day we get fresh snow.

SOMETIMES IT'S NOT JUST ABOUT THE VOLUME

Just as it is in humans, inflammation associated with urinary tract infections makes dogs feel like they have to pee ALL THE TIME.

I had a UTI once and I still remember the living hell of having to take a daily long bus trip to school (with no toilet on the bus)

A dog with a UTI is most likely going to urinate frequently and small amounts. There can also be blood in the urine. Accidents are likely to appear on the way to the door.

With some medical conditions, urination can be painful, and a dog will avoid urinating until they cannot hold it anymore.

Dogs who are suffering from obesity, arthritis, pain, stiffness or neurological issues will also sometimes alter their body posture, leading to urine retention and a predisposition towards UTIs. Some infections do not cause symptoms, and regular urine checks are a good idea in these cases.

Jasmine got her first-ever UTI after her neck injury when her mobility was affected.

If your dog is straining to urinate and the urine stream looks thin or weak, see your vet as soon as possible.

Urinary tract obstruction is a medical emergency.

The cause of the blockage can be stones in the urinary tract, injuries, tumors, or prostate disease (in male dogs).

Urinary incontinence, even though it can also be associated with a urinary tract infection, is often another issue altogether.

True urinary incontinence is caused by a dog's inability to prevent their bladder from leaking. This is most commonly caused by poor control of the sphincter leading out of the bladder.

Obesity is a common risk factor. Spayed female dogs can develop urinary incontinence associated with low estrogen levels, which leads to weakening of the sphincter muscle.

Other causes include congenital abnormalities, neurological issues, and spinal cord injuries or degeneration.

Only after all of the various medical problems have been ruled out can a dog's "accidents" be blamed on a behavioral problem, most of which are associated with some form of anxiety or fear.

Punishment is never the answer to inappropriate peeing... Your dog is either sick or scared.

THE PEE DICTIONARY

Polyuria (increased volume of urine)	Associated with renal dysfunction which may be either a primary problem with the kidneys or secondary to something else such as diabetes
Pollakiuria (increased urination frequency)	Most commonly associated with urinary tract infections
Urinary incontinence (not being able to hold the pee)	Most commonly urinary sphincter mechanism incontinence and most common in females

WHEN IS IT AN EMERGENCY?

Any dog that is straining to urinate should be considered an emergency until proven otherwise. Excessive urination is unlikely to be an emergency, but any other symptoms present need to be taken into account.

WHAT'S IN THE URINE?

To a dog, urine isn't just waste; it is a precious commodity. I'm always fascinated by how carefully our dogs select just the right spot worthy of their deposit.

I'm sure that you have noticed your dog's fascination with urine markings. It is imperative that every tree, every pole and every hydrant gets carefully examined.

You might think that dogs can't read but they can! Only their required reading isn't written in words.

"If reading scents is for dogs the equivalent of reading a written message, then the canine equivalent of ink is urine."

—Stanley Coren, How to Speak Dog

Leaving urine markings, to dogs, is like sending out a resume.

DOGS GET SO MUCH INFORMATION FROM URINE, AND WE CAN TOO!

Examining your dog's urine can provide a great deal of information about their physical condition and health. Changes in urination and urine quality can not only indicate problems within the urinary tract itself, but also systemic disease.

URINATION FREQUENCY, PAINFUL URINATION OR LOSS OF THE ABILITY TO HOLD URINE

Excessive urination (polyuria), usually combined with excessive drinking (polydipsia), is an important symptom that can signal a number of health problems, such as diabetes, Cushing's disease, Addison's disease, kidney or liver failure, and infection.[20] (Bladder infections rarely cause true polyuria. However, kidney infections can).

Straining to urinate (dysuria)[21] can be caused by urinary tract obstruction, tumors, bladder stones or prostate disease (in males). The number one cause of dysuria is probably a bladder infection.[22]

Urinary tract obstruction (not being able to pass urine despite straining) is an emergency situation and requires immediate veterinary care.

Urinary incontinence is a condition most often seen in older dogs, but it can happen at any age. It is most common in spayed females, though it can affect male dogs also. It is usually caused by hormonal deficiencies and/or loss of control of the urethral sphincter (the muscle that closes the bladder). However, anatomical, structural or neurological abnormalities of the urinary tract can be responsible also.

Your dog might also be unable to hold their urine as a result of excessive drinking (see above), or a urinary tract infection.

20 http://www.petplace.com/article/dogs/diseases-conditions-of-dogs/symptoms/polydipsia-and-polyuria-excessive-drinking-and-urinating-in-dogs
21 http://www.petmd.com/dog/conditions/urinary/c_multi_urinary_tract_obstruction
22 http://www.petplace.com/article/dogs/diseases-conditions-of-dogs/symptoms/dysuria-trouble-urinating-in-dogs

It is important to distinguish between polyuria, dysuria, and urinary incontinence because each symptom has its own set of potential causes.

With polyuria, your dog will produce large volumes of urine and may urinate quite frequently. Dogs suffering from polyuria may not be able to hold their urine for long periods of time. Polyuria is accompanied by polydipsia (increased water consumption.) Dogs with polyuria also usually produce very dilute urine which may be clear or have a very light yellow coloration.

By contrast, dogs suffering from dysuria generally urinate quite frequently but produce only small amounts of urine each time. In some cases, blood may be observed, depending on the cause of the dysuria.

Dogs with urinary incontinence lose the ability to be able to control their urinary habits. They urinate involuntarily and sometimes unknowingly. Frequently these dogs will leave wet spots where they have been sleeping or resting. They may also dribble urine while awake. Often, the dog is totally unaware that the urination is happening.

Differentiating between these symptoms can sometimes be difficult. It may not be possible to tell for certain at home exactly what is happening.

Your veterinarian can help determine whether your dog is suffering from polyuria, dysuria or urinary incontinence by asking you questions and performing a physical examination and a urinalysis.

WHAT'S IN THE COLOR?

Normal urine should be clear and light yellow to light amber in color.

Pale or clear urine could mean over-hydration, but it can also indicate kidney disease or other conditions that interfere with urine concentration.

A single episode of pale or clear urine is usually not significant, particularly if your dog just "tanked up" from the water bowl. However, a persistently pale or clear color usually indicates dilute urine and may be due to the kidney's inability to concentrate the urine for a variety of causes. This is especially true if dilute urine is accompanied by greater than normal desire to drink water.

Dark yellow usually signals dehydration. Again, one dark pee, no dark pee. However, persistently dark urine may indicate a problem and warrants a trip to the veterinarian.

Dark yellow urine particularly when accompanied by other symptoms of illness such as a lack of appetite, lethargy, vomiting or diarrhea is a cause for concern and will require a veterinary visit.

Urine that has a color other than shades of yellow is always bad news. Red, orange or brown discoloration can be a sign of bleeding into the urinary tract, damage to red blood cells, liver disease or the breakdown of muscle fibers.

Your dog may have blood in his or her urine for many different reasons. Bladder infections can cause bloody urine as can bladder stones, tumors, and other diseases.

BLADDER INFECTIONS, PARTICULARLY IF RECURRENT OR NOT RESPONSIVE TO TREATMENT, MAY BE A SYMPTOM OF A LARGER PROBLEM.

Bladder stones (also known as cystic calculi or uroliths) come in several different types. Struvite stones are most often associated with infection and are not likely to resolve until the infection is controlled and the stones are dissolved with special foods or medications to acidify the urine. Calcium oxalate stones are sometimes seen when the pH of urine is higher than normal. In Dalmatians, urate stones are common. Stones of mixed composition may be seen in some dogs. Identification of the type of stone present is important to choose the correct treatment option (e.g., surgery versus medical dissolution) and a prevention plan.

If your dog's urine is red, orange or brown, you want to see your veterinarian as soon as possible.

Orange or brown colored urine can be caused by bilirubin or myoglobin in the urine. Bilirubin may be present in the urine if your dog's liver is not functioning normally or if your dog is suffering from the widespread destruction of red blood cells, such as is seen in Autoimmune Hemolytic Anemia (AIHA). Myoglobin is released from muscles when they are severely damaged as can occur in cases of heat stroke.

Cloudy urine likely signals bladder infection. However, bladder infections might not always cause cloudiness. A foul or musty odor may sometimes, but not always, be detected in the urine in cases of urinary tract infections also. Cloudiness can also be caused by the abnormal presence of sugar, protein, fat or crystals in the urine.

Foamy urine can be a sign of excess protein in the urine which is sometimes a symptom of kidney failure.

Most owners try to have as little to do with their dog's urine as possible, but looking for changes in urinary habits and urine characteristics is an excellent way to monitor your dog's health.

THINK LIKE A DOG AND LEARN TO READ THE PEE!

In the end, all you need to be able to figure out is whether your dog needs to see a vet and how soon.

Your vet is much better at reading your dog's urine—after all, they've got the tools! Urinalysis is the technical term for a thorough examination of urine.

URINALYSIS

Veterinarians often recommend a urinalysis when presented with a dog with changes in their urinary or drinking habits, change in the characteristics (e.g., color) of a dog's urine, if a dog seems to be "off" in any way, or as part of wellness screening.

If it sounds like veterinarians are willing to run a urinalysis at the drop of a hat... that's a good thing!

A urinalysis is inexpensive, noninvasive, and provides a wealth of information about a dog's well-being.

CONTAMINATED OR STALE PEE IS USELESS PEE

To obtain useful information from a urinalysis, the sample needs to be fresh and uncontaminated. For most purposes, to collect a sample, you can simply catch the urine in a clean container as your dog pees. It's not always as easy as it sounds, although we became quite skillful at collecting Jasmine's. Haven't had to try with JD yet, but I bet it is harder trying to catch it from a boy.

It is important that you use a dry, clean container. A dirty old yogurt jar might come back with some impressive results. Don't laugh; this happens more frequently than you think. We usually collect a sample right in front of the vet's office; dogs love to sniff around and make sure that all future visitors know they've been there.

SOMETIMES ABSOLUTE STERILITY IS CRUCIAL

A urine sample can also be collected by your veterinarian using a catheter or by cystocentesis (a needle inserted into the bladder).

This will ensure a fresh and uncontaminated sample but ouch! So far we've always gotten away with free catch samples. We weren't looking for infections, though. When the vet is worried about the possibility of infection, the sterility of the sample is critical.

Now that your vet has the sample, they can evaluate the urine.

INFORMATION YOUR VET CAN GET FROM THE PEE

The first step is similar to what you might have observed yourself. The sample will be examined for color and cloudiness.

Next step two is to measure the Urine Specific Gravity (USG), which indicates the concentration of the urine. USG tests the ability of the kidneys to concentrate or dilute urine, in other words, their ability to function.

Dilute urine could simply mean over-hydration, but it can also indicate kidney disease or other conditions that interfere with urine concentration.

Overly concentrated urine can be caused by dehydration or other problems.

A chemical analysis is a number of chemical tests performed using a dipstick (a specially coated test strip) or a special instrument.

The following tests are usually included in the chemical analysis:

Urine pH may be influenced by diet, and an abnormally high or low pH can be behind the formation of bladder stones or crystals.

I remember stalking Jasmine with a collection jar and a pH test strip, checking her urine a couple of times a day, when urine acidity was a suspect for some of her issues at that time.

Glucose in urine is often a sign of diabetes mellitus or stress.

Protein levels are measured to determine whether there is kidney damage or inflammation in the urinary tract.

Ketones in the urine are usually associated with diabetes mellitus.

Excess bilirubin can be a sign of liver disease.

Other chemical tests may be included in some types of urine dipsticks.

Finally, a centrifuge is used to separate sediment, which is then further evaluated under a microscope.

A higher than normal number of red blood cells in urine can be caused by a number of issues, such as trauma, urinary tract inflammation or infection, bladder stones or blood clotting problems.

The presence of white blood cells may indicate inflammation or infection.

Observing bacteria can indicate infection as long as the sample was taken using sterile technique. The urine can then be cultured to determine the type of bacteria present and which antibiotics should be most effective against them.

Crystals in the urine can be seen with bladder stones.

A special type of urinalysis can also be used to help screen for Cushing's disease. Cortisol : creatinine ratio is measured. While this test is not conclusive for Cushing's disease, affected dogs will usually have abnormal results. We used it to get a better idea of what might be behind Jasmine's issues. To confirm such a diagnosis, specialized testing needs to be performed.

***

Just as with any other diagnostic tool, urinalysis is open to interpretation and further testing might be required if the findings are inconclusive.

It is important that the results are viewed in light of a dog's medical history, physical exam and other diagnostic tests.

Lethargy

lethargy [ˈleTHərjē] – lack of energy and enthusiasm; state of sleepiness or deep unresponsiveness and inactivity

One of the most ambiguous and yet extremely important symptoms to watch for in dogs is lethargy.

THE QUIETER YOUR DOG GETS, THE MORE SERIOUS THE SITUATION IS

This is one of the times when knowing what is normal for your dog is paramount. If JD spends most of the day laying by the window watching out for traffic to bark at, it's perfectly normal for him. He likes a good short run, and after that, he's happy to relax.

When Cookie wants to rest after a short run, I know something is up. For her to be content, she needs her daily activity dose of three hours running, playing and hunting.

The times when Jasmine wasn't all excited going for her walk, she was seriously ill.

A puppy that is not up to playing is an emergency.

WHAT IS GOING ON?

Unfortunately, the fact that your dog is lethargic doesn't tell you anything about the reason behind it. Lethargy is a very nonspecific sign that gives you no idea of the cause but is something you need to take seriously. Even when lack of energy is the only thing you notice.

Anything that will cause your dog unwell can result in lethargy.

This is why when your dog becomes severely lethargic, or the lethargy persists for more than a day or two, you do need to see a veterinarian.

LETHARGY IS A MAJOR RED FLAG

One day Cookie woke up in the morning and was quite lethargic. Given her normal disposition, this was alarming. The first thing I did was to check her vitals, her gums, and look for the presence of any other warning signs.

Other than the lethargy and disinterest in food, there were none. Everything seemed normal, and we were quite certain she didn't get into anything poisonous or get bitten or stung by anything. If I had found one more worrisome sign, though, we'd have been on our way to the emergency clinic. Because Cookie otherwise looked good, and it was Sunday, and the vet was closed, we decided to give her a bit of time to get over whatever was wrong. She improved by the end of the day. If she didn't, we'd had been on our way to the vet the next morning.

The only other time Cookie was lethargic like that was when she got pancreatitis. She looked *beat*. Too beat for any reasonable explanation. Lethargy was the first sign; which came well before refusing to eat and any vomiting and diarrhea cropping up.

A friend's dog seemed a bit listless and lethargic one night. By morning she was barely able to stand, and her skin turned a pale, yellowish color. She had Immune-Mediated Hemolytic Anemia (IMHA). Because they acted quickly, the dog survived. But with things like this, time is of the essence. Lethargy, together with pale gums, is serious. Be on your way to a vet.

CONDITIONS THAT CAN CAUSE LETHARGY IN DOGS

- Trauma
- Poisoning
- Pain
- Infections
- Hypoglycemia (low blood sugar)
- Anemia or other blood disorders
- Heart disease
- Respiratory conditions
- Liver disease
- Diabetes mellitus
- Hypothyroidism
- Addison's disease
- Cancer
- Certain medications
- Snake bites
- Parasites
- Dehydration
- Hypothermia
- Gastrointestinal problems
- Urinary tract problems
- Electrolyte abnormalities
- Immune diseases
- Neurological and neuromuscular disorders
- Certain eye diseases
- Musculoskeletal diseases

You see, I wasn't kidding when I said that virtually any problem at all could cause your dog to become lethargic.

GRADUAL CHANGE

One trap that's easy to fall into is when changes happen gradually over time.

When your active and playful dog suddenly becomes lethargic, you *know* something is wrong.

But what if your dog slowly becomes quieter and quieter, over time? Such gradual changes are easy to miss.

You might think your dog is just slowing down with age. But I have seen senior dogs who could outplay the youngest of them. It is not age that will slow your dog down; it is most likely pain or another medical problem. Always keep that in mind.

When your dog becomes lethargic, he is talking to you. He is saying, "I feel like crap, please, do something." It's the equivalent of a person saying, "I think I should see a doctor."

WHEN IS IT AN EMERGENCY?

While it is difficult to put a scale on something like this, to me this is one of the most serious symptoms. My dogs are active and loving life; if they become lethargic I know something is wrong. Any significant lethargy sends me on the way to a vet. A sudden onset of letharcy is likely to be an emergency.

There are times when severe lethargy might be the only warning you get. Things like immune-mediated hemolytic anemia (IMHA), internal bleeding whether from trauma or splenic tumor, severe fever, sepsis ... are all conditions where time is of the essence.

Loss of Appetite

Loss of appetite is one of the most unappreciated symptoms, particularly when the dog eats some or is thought to be a picky eater. For the longest time, we believed that Jasmine just wasn't so interested in food …

IS THERE SUCH AS THING AS A DOG THAT ISN'T SO INTERESTED IN FOOD?

Some small breed dogs might be notorious for being picky eaters. But generally, I believe that if a dog doesn't want to eat, there is something really wrong with the food or something is medically wrong with the dog.

DOGS LOVE TO EAT!

Getting enough food is a question of survival. Instinct drives dogs to eat and eating brings satisfaction. Dogs are considered opportunistic scavengers: When there is an opportunity to eat something, they will. If they don't, I get concerned.

WHEN A DOG DOESN'T WANT TO EAT, SOMETHING IS AMISS.

Yes, I believe a dog can become a *picky eater*, particularly after getting a taste of something especially yummy, or in efforts to manipulate their owners into feeding them particular food, or at least served to them on their terms.

My mom's parents had a dog for a short while. They fed him risotto type food. Some rice, some veggies, some bits of meat. He was perfectly adept at picking out the meat and leaving the rest.

At that time, my mom kept rabbits for food. For one reason or another, she ended up with way too much rabbit meat and so she gave some to her parents. It was too much for them too, so a bunch of it went to the dog. He didn't complain in the least.

When they ran out of the rabbit meat, though, he was determined not to go back to what he considered an *inferior diet*. He refused food for a week until he finally got hungry enough to give in! He was clearly on a hunger strike, demanding more of the good stuff.

In Jasmine's case, it turned out that all that time she was suffering from food allergies and IBD, which her vets missed for five years. Once she was finally diagnosed and the problem was addressed, you should have seen her polish her bowl off in no time!

Every now and then, she didn't want her dinner, and we knew that her IBD was acting up.

The only time Cookie refused food was when she had a bout of pancreatitis after getting into some horse feed. JD only missed a meal to throw up a bunch of plastic later on.

Every time we have had a dog not eating, there has been an actual reason behind it.

FINICKY EATERS AND DECREASED APPETITE

Yes, there can be an issue with the food. Taking a good look at the diet isn't a bad idea. Perhaps it isn't palatable. Maybe the fat in it went rancid. Or their system doesn't tolerate a particular ingredient. Some dogs also seem to have a definite preference when it comes to consistency (canned versus kibble).

But if I found myself embellishing what I give my dog in escalating frequency until they won't eat anything other than fillet mignon, I'd give the situation a second thought.

PERHAPS THE DOG DOESN'T FEEL WELL, AND ONLY THE MOST ENTICING FOODS CAN CONVINCE THEM TO EAT

Before I'd accept that my dog was simply picky, I'd want to rule out every other possible reason for their poor appetite.

STRESS, FEAR, AND ANXIETY CAN CAUSE DECREASED APPETITE

Don't I know it. Every time something isn't right with any of our dogs, I just can't force myself to eat anything. It can happen to a dog too.

There is even a biological explanation for that. Enough stress keeps the body in fight or flight mode. All other functions are suspended. Did you ever try running away from danger while munching on a burger? I'm sure the burger is the first thing you let go of.

Stress is a real problem. Prolonged stress can do a lot of damage to a dog's body. If your dog is stressed enough to refuse food, he needs some serious help.

VIRTUALLY ANY HEALTH PROBLEM WILL MESS WITH APPETITE

Some medical conditions can cause voracious appetite. Most of the time, though, appetite will decrease. The problem can be within the digestive system itself or elsewhere in the body. Some of the medical causes of decreased appetite include:

- Upsets within the digestive tract
- Intestinal parasites or infection
- Intestinal obstruction (partial or complete)

- Inflammatory bowel disease
- Gastrointestinal foreign bodies
- Problems with the pancreas
- Liver disease
- Kidney disease
- Heart disease
- Cancer
- Neurological problems
- Toxicities and medications
- Metabolic diseases
- Immune disorders
- Infections/fever
- Pain
- Hematologic (blood) diseases
- Dental disease (though you'd be quite surprised how bad the mouth can be and the dog still eating!)
- Dehydration

Every time any of our dogs had a change in appetite, there was a medical reason for it. Some of those are more serious than others. Some might require immediate attention, particularly if your dog stops eating altogether.

The situation becomes more urgent when other symptoms come with it, such as vomiting, diarrhea, lethargy, weakness, difficulty breathing, increased thirst and urination, rapid weight loss ... When your dog's appetite tanks, take it seriously.

WHEN IS IT AN EMERGENCY?

Complete loss of appetite is a major red flag in most dogs. While generally not an emergency in itself, it can be a sign of an impending one. It can become an emergency with puppies, tiny dogs, dogs on certain medications such as NSAIDs, or dogs with known systemic disease.

Changes in Behavior

Changes in behavior are probably the most misunderstood of all symptoms. In fact, most of the time they are not considered a symptom at all.

EVERY CHANGE IS SIGNIFICANT AND MEANS SOMETHING.

Did your normally friendly and playful dog suddenly become grouchy and snappy? Did your dog stop enjoying going for walks? Did your dog suddenly start seeking places to hide, looking to be left alone? Has your dog stopped listening to you? Does your dog no longer get on the bed with you? Does your dog pace around all night? Did your dog start licking at the air and everything in sight?

PAIN IS THE NUMBER ONE REASON

The most common cause behind changes in behavior or routine is pain.

Whether it is from an injury or a disease, you don't want your dog to suffer.

Before we found out about Jasmine's arthritis and bad knees, she started refusing JD's rough play. She got grumpy when he got into her space when resting. We thought it was because he was rather obnoxious, which he was back then. She lost interest in chew toys and stopped fetching a ball but would fetch flatter objects such as the Flying Squirrel. That's because she had arthritis in her jaw too.

Back then, we didn't understand these changes.

To further complicate things, she'd been at the vet often enough that we figured if something were wrong the vet would have alerted us. But many of our concerns were dismissed.

When I learned to pay closer attention, my frustration grew even higher. At one time Jasmine started burying her pee. No, I don't mean ground-scoring, I mean trying to cover up her pee by pushing dirt on it with her nose. Her vet at the time was not listening to me. He just kept repeating that it was normal. Ground-scoring is normal, yes. But that's not what she was doing. I was unable to get through to him.

It wasn't until later, with a new vet and Jasmine's IBD diagnosis and treatment, that she stopped doing that and started to score the ground instead. We always celebrated when we saw that behavior because to us it was evidence of her positive self-assessment.

SOME CHANGES ARE MORE OBVIOUS THAN OTHERS

Some changes scream out loud, such as aggression, while others whisper quietly, such as seeking quiet, not jumping up on your bed anymore, or disinterest in play.

Sometimes a new behavior might even appear to be a welcome change, such as a dog resting more instead of bouncing off the walls or no longer running along the fence and barking at anything that goes by.

AGGRESSION AND IRRITABILITY ARE A COMMON CAUSE OF CONCERN

Any condition causing pain or discomfort can lead to an increase in irritability or anxiety/fear of being approached or handled. A dog with impaired hearing or vision can snap when startled and might become more irritable because the world has become a much scarier place.

Rabies should not be ignored as a potential cause of behavior changes.

WEAKNESS OR LETHARGY

Towards the end of his life, Bruin started ignoring us when we asked him to do something. He'd just lay there and stare. Loss of hearing could result in disobedience, but his hearing was fine. It wasn't until he got to the point that we knew the end was near when we learned what was happening. We took him to the clinic thinking it was his time; indeed it was. His heart was so weak the vet couldn't even detect a pulse. Poor Bruin just didn't have the energy to do what we were asking of him.

CIRCLING

Circling can be brought on by a middle ear infection, vestibular disease, stroke or other neurological problem, liver failure, Cushing's disease ... basically, anything that has an adverse effect on the brain.

PRESSING HEAD INTO CORNERS

This is a sign consistent with severe neurological disorders, or head trauma. See a vet immediately if your dog starts head pressing.

PANTING, PACING, RESTLESSNESS

At the age of two Jasmine started having episodes of panting and pacing around the house. We took her to the vet so many times trying to nail down the cause. Everything was considered and ruled out. After all said and done, I think her bad neck might have been the cause all along. But that only made sense in the light of her last days.

While anxiety is a common cause, these behaviors can be a sign of pain, discomfort, or emotional distress, such as that caused by canine cognitive dysfunction or other neurological problems.

Remember, these signs can also be the earliest sign of bloat, which is the mother of all emergencies.

CHANGES IN APPETITE

While you might be tempted to celebrate when your "chow hound" loses his fixation on food or your picky eater begins eating everything in sight, changes in appetite are associated with a long list of disorders ranging from dental disease to GI conditions to hormonal imbalances.

EXCESSIVE LICKING OF SURFACES

For a long time considered an obsessive-compulsive disorder, this behavior was recently linked with GI disorders, ranging from giardiasis, chronic pancreatitis, and many other problems.

LOSS OF HOUSEBREAKING

A dog who suddenly starts having accidents in the house is not being "bad" but is usually suffering from a urinary or digestive disorder, neurological disease, or anxiety. Punishing a dog for having an accident when he or she is truly sick or scared is cruel and ineffective.

I cannot list all the possibilities here, but the rule of thumb with any change is to always look for a medical reason before assuming that the cause is purely behavioral.

Know what is normal for your dog, be a keen observer and investigate the cause no matter how deep you might have to dig.

WHEN IS IT AN EMERGENCY?

While in general changes in behavior are not an emergency, let your instinct guide you. Abrupt, dramatic change in behavior with or without other signs can mean an emergency.

- pressing head in corners
- extreme lethargy
- painful behaviors
- restlessness/inability to get comfortable

Limping

Even the healthiest dogs will likely end up limping at some point of their lives.

IF YOUR DOG IS LIMPING, THERE IS PAIN

Many people think that their dog is *just limping,* but he's not in pain. Why else would they be limping then? When was the last time you limped for some philosophical reason and not because of pain?

It is the same with dogs. They'll limp because it hurts. This is important to realize and address.

IT SEEMS PRETTY STRAIGHTFORWARD

They're limping because of a sore leg, such as a pulled muscle, right? Perhaps.

Your past experience will influence what you read into a limp. Beware of the assumption trap.

EXPERIENCES BREED BIAS

After Jasmine having had to have surgery on both of her knees, when I see a limp on a hind leg, a knee injury is the first thing that comes to mind. It is true that torn cruciate ligament is one of the most common injuries in dogs. But it's by far not the only reason for hind leg lameness.

With no more cruciate ligaments to rupture, Jasmine presented us with a limp that looked exactly the same. How could that be? How likely is it that the surgically repaired knee would go bad again after fully healed? Not likely at all.

THERE ARE MANY DIFFERENT REASONS WHY YOUR DOG MIGHT BECOME LAME[23]

Start by trying to figure out which leg has the problem. This is not always as easy as it sounds. Observe your dog carefully. Whenever possible, dogs will try to reduce the amount of weight they put on a painful leg.

LAMENESS IS NOT AN EMERGENCY UNLESS ...

If your dog is not bearing any weight on the affected limb, and particularly if they're also crying, seek veterinary help right away. Ignoring a serious injury can lead to complications that could have been avoided.

In less serious cases, examine the affected leg thoroughly, starting from the toes and working your way upward. You might find a lesion, rock, splinter or something else minor causing major lameness.

Sometimes seemingly small things can cause a substantial lameness

A chunk of a porcupine quill in Cookie's foot resulted in complete lameness of her hind left leg. She wouldn't bear any weight on it at all. It looked very much like a busted knee. I could have sworn that's what it was.

No matter what you think might be going on, take a moment to examine your dog.

Jasmine's foot infection also caused her to favor the affected leg some.

---

23 http://www.peteducation.com/article.cfm?c=2+2084&aid=241

A cracked or split nail can be very painful and cause substantial lameness. Cracks that bleed might require sedation to be properly taken care of. Bruised or fractured toes, cut webbing or pads, foreign objects wedged between the toes, masses or cysts can all also cause your dog to limp.

Quite a list already and we didn't even get past the feet, huh?

If the feet check out, continue to examine along the leg. Look for any swelling, grazes or bruising, heat, pain when being touched, bleeding or asymmetry. Carefully compare with the other leg. Try to determine where the pain is originating from.

A friend's dog started limping suddenly on his hind leg, and they too assumed it was an injured knee. It turned out being a snake or spider bite. So always pay attention and be thorough. Depending on the type of snake or spider, their bite can be very dangerous.

Not bearing any weight on the affected leg could also mean a broken bone; obviously, these injuries are extremely painful and harder to repair the longer they are left untreated.

Last but not least are the joints. Injuries, structural abnormalities or flare-ups of chronic conditions, such as arthritis, can all cause lameness. Joint problems that can result in a limp include cruciate ligament tears, hip dysplasia, luxating patella, elbow dysplasia, osteochondritis dissecans, arthritis and other conditions.

And while scaring you is not my intention, the most serious cause of pain and lameness is bone cancer.

Typically, in young dogs, the most common causes of lameness are strains, sprains or bruises, and in older dogs joint issues. But that does not always have to be the case.

Tip: if your dog's lameness is worst in the morning, you're likely looking at a joint problem, while lameness at the end of the day could point to a muscle problem.

It is important to recognize when simply resting your dog is appropriate and when you should seek veterinary attention.

If your dog is in extreme pain, has been limping for an extended period of time and rest isn't helping, if there is bleeding or suspicious lumps or swelling, please see your veterinarian as soon as possible.

To complicate matters further, there are situations when your dog's limping might have nothing to do with the limbs at all.

There was one time when Jasmine came home from the horse farm completely lame on her hind right leg. She wouldn't put any weight on it at all, even when lying down. It looked even worse than when she had torn her knee ligament.

We took her to her chiropractor/physical therapist.

There was a tweaked area in the spine, which was causing the lameness.

After one chiropractic adjustment, the limp was gone. When Jasmine started having problems with her neck, one of the ways it presented itself was also front leg lameness.

As you see, simple limping might not always be so simple and sometimes it can be a symptom of a serious problem.

While rest might often be all your dog needs, please be observant and diligent and take limping seriously.

WHEN IS IT AN EMERGENCY?

Limping generally is not an emergency unless

- there has been a major trauma
- there is fraction or dislocation, bleeding, severe swelling, hot limbs or dragging of limbs
- there is severe pain

Lumps and Bumps

"Can anybody tell me what that bump/lump/swelling is on my dog?" This is one of the most frequent questions owners ask... some include a photo and some figure a description should be enough.

Certainly, they get kudos for finding it.

That is the most important step - discovering the bump/lump. That is one of the reasons why regular grooming, brushing and running your hands all over your dog's body is a vital part of their care.

THE SECOND MOST IMPORTANT STEP IS HAVING IT IDENTIFIED

And they realize that, which is why they post to ask about it or search online photos. But is that the right way to go about it?

First, many of the online photos that might look like the bump you found on your dog are mislabeled. Even if you find one that looks exactly like what your dog has, there is no guarantee that it is what the source says it is.

Secondly, just because the photo does look right and assuming it is labeled correctly, it still doesn't mean that is what your dog has.

With rare exceptions, nobody, not even a board-certified oncologist, can identify a lump just by looking at it.

HAS THE LUMP/BUMP/SWELLING HAS APPEARED SUDDENLY?

Are you sure it has appeared suddenly? Often people swear it wasn't there the day before. Hubby always says, "I know that you're sure, but are you right?"

A lump/swelling that suddenly pops up can be caused by a sting, bite or an infection. This may or may not be an emergency but requires veterinary attention unless it disappears on its own within a day or two.

MOST LUMPS AND BUMPS HAVE LIKELY BEEN THERE MUCH LONGER THAN YOU THINK

They are particularly hard to find when they are tiny. But even a large lump can go unnoticed. When we adopted Bruin, he got his initial thorough vet exam, and nothing was found amiss. Yet, I thought his chest looked weird. Nobody else agreed, saying that's just the way his chest looks (he was a big boy.) It wasn't until one day at the farm when hubby called me all panicked that Bruin has this HUGE lump that appeared *all of the sudden*.

IT WAS SIZE OF A BASEBALL; IT DID NOT JUST APPEAR OVERNIGHT

What happened instead is that it was sitting there the whole time, evenly distributed across the chest. As Bruin started to thin out, it must have gotten loose and moved to the side. NOW it was really obvious. Fortunately, it turned out to be a lipoma, a benign fatty tumor.

FINDING A BUMP ON YOUR DOG IS SCARY, AND DENIAL IS TEMPTING

But denial never cured anything. The best policy when you find a bump is to have it examined AND identified. If it is harmless, fantastic, at least you know. If it isn't, at least you can do something about it. The sooner it gets treated, the better.

Lumps and bumps on dogs range from pimples, warts, abscesses and histiocytomas to fatty tumors, mast cell tumors and many other cancerous growths.

SEE SOMETHING, DO SOMETHING

When I found a lump on Jasmine's nipple, we took her to the vet right away. He was reasonably sure it was an infection, and a short course of antibiotics cleared it right up. But we did SOMETHING.

Breast cancer in dogs is quite common and aggressive.

If this had been cancer, catching and removing it early could have been the difference between life and death.

NOBODY KNOWS WHAT A BUMP IS UNLESS THEY LOOK AT THE CELLS

Dr. Sue Ettinger, a veterinary oncologist, launched a campaign to educate owners as well as veterinarians, to raise cancer awareness and promote early detection. The simple rule is that if a lump on your dog is the size of a pea or larger, or it has been there for a month, see a vet.

Having it checked doesn't mean your vet taking a look and proposing the wait and see approach. Wait for what? Cancer to grow and spread?

DON'T WAIT, ASPIRATE

The only way to correctly identify a lump is to take a look at the cells inside it, which means a needle aspirate or a biopsy. Why? The fact that it might look like one thing or another does not make it one thing or another.

When we found a small bump on JD's leg, at first we figured it might be a bit of swelling or infection from having a run-in with a branch or stump. We kept an eye on it for a couple of weeks to see if it would change or go away. It didn't, and so we decided it was time to aspirate.

The vet checked it out and figured it was probably a cyst. I had them to aspirate it anyway. To a plain eye, even the material on the slide looked like it came from a cyst. But it wasn't. When the biopsy results came back, the lump was identified as a mast cell tumor.

MEASURE TWICE, CUT ONCE

Jumping the gun and having a lump removed without proper identification is a double-edged sword. You can end up with not enough tissue removed and cancerous cells left behind. This only results in more treatment and more risk to your dog.

Knowing what JD's mass was, we knew our aim was getting clean margins. In other words, removing enough tissue that all cancer cells are out.

Because of the location, this wasn't an easy task because there isn't much tissue there to start with. It could happen that there wouldn't be enough tissue left to close the wound. We discussed it thoroughly and decided that clean margins were a priority. JD ended up having to get a skin graft, but we did get it all out, and it was well worth that.

BACK TO THE LAB

After the removed tissue was examined, we did get clean margins. Only healthy cells remained. It is important not to leave "cancer seeds" behind.

MORE THAN HALF OF LUMPS AND BUMPS ARE NOT CANCEROUS

That sounds comforting, but I wouldn't take a gamble with a guess. Do it *by the book*; then you'll know. And once you know you can either celebrate or take appropriate action.

WHEN IS IT AN EMERGENCY?

Lumps and bumps are usually not an emergency. Rarely, an abscess or boil may require urgent care. However, if there is any chance a lump could have been caused by a snake, spider or insect bite, that requires prompt veterinary care.

Excessive Head Shaking

You might have noticed that when talking about symptoms, sometimes I use a qualifying word such as excessive panting, excessive drinking, excessive head shaking ... That's because these are normal behaviors and whether or not there is a problem is a question of degree.

A dog will shake their head in response to discomfort, pain or irritation. This can be as benign as a little itch, tickle or a bug bite, or as serious as inflammation or infection.

If my dog is shaking their head, persistently I look for a cause.

On our summer walks, JD shakes his head often, to fend off bugs. Deer flies, in particular, seem to like him. I think they know they can drive him nuts. Jasmine was much less concerned about them, and they left her mostly alone.

One day, on the way from the farm, JD kept shaking his head incessantly even though he was already in the truck where there were no insects.

We were going to check his ears first thing when we got home. He kept shaking and shaking ... and then we saw an ant waltz out of his ear. There was our culprit. The shaking stopped.

When a tick got a bite on Jasmine's ear, her instinct was to shake her head. The bite was painful for Jasmine, and every time she shook her head she'd cry a little, stop and hold her head down, tilted towards the affected ear.

We immediately started examining the ear and found and removed the invader.

When your dog starts shaking their head like that, check the ears, eyes, head, neck and skin carefully. Pay particularly close attention to the ears.

A common cause of head shaking is otitis externa, inflammation of the ear canal. Grass awns, ear mites or allergies can be behind an unhappy ear. An inflamed ear makes a great playground for bacteria or yeast. Infection often follows.

If there is redness, swelling, discharge or a bad odor to the ears, it's time to see your veterinarian. If pain is involved, see your veterinarian right away. If you have a reason to suspect a foxtail, also don't delay. Those nasty little things can make their way through tissues and cause serious damage.

Some breeds are also susceptible to ear vasculitis, which is inflammation of the blood vessels in the ear flap.

Dogs with balance issues, be it from trauma, stroke, inner ear infection or vestibular syndrome, might shake their heads in an attempt to relieve their symptoms.

Not only does excessive head shaking indicate a problem, but it can also cause one as well.

Sometimes a dog can shake their head so much that it will cause the blood vessels in the ear flap to rupture, resulting in a hematoma. The swelling is quite apparent.

A hematoma is a pocket of blood, and it will cause your dog to shake their head even more. Ear hematomas require veterinary attention if they are to heal without permanent disfigurement.

What I described above refers to voluntary head shaking. There is also such a thing as involuntary head tremors, which are another story altogether.

WHEN IS IT AN EMERGENCY?

Violent head shaking can be caused by an injury to the ear and I would treated as an emergency particularly if the dog is clearly in pain or the ear is bleeding.

Head Tilting

There is the adorable head tilt that dogs do when you talk to them. And then there is the head tilt that is a sign of a problem.

WHICH IS WHICH?

The head tilt we all love can vary from side to side, in response to interesting stimuli. The dog is looking at the source of the stimulus and is happy and intrigued. When whatever was interesting stops, so does the head tilt.

A PERSISTENT HEAD TILT TO ONLY ONE SIDE NEEDS YOUR ATTENTION

It is quite easy to recognize that something is going on.

Your dog might also have problems with balance, walk in circles, their eyes might be flicking back and forth (nystagmus), and show other signs of a problem.

Once Jasmine gave us quite a scare when she suddenly started walking funny, holding her head low, tilting it to one side and whimpering. It came out of the blue, and she looked very unhappy.

First, we checked her ear on the affected side. And there it was. She had a tick latched to her ear flap.

Jasmine wasn't a crybaby; I assume that it might have bitten her right at a nerve ending and causing substantial pain. Just recently there was a story about a dog becoming very lame because a tick attached to his foot.

PAIN OR DISCOMFORT CAN CAUSE A DOG TO TILT THEIR HEAD LIKE THAT

Cookie does that when something is bothering her ear, such as deer fly bite or itch.

The tilt goes away as soon as the problem is addressed, and I don't panic every time my dog tilts their head temporarily. However, there are more serious things that can be behind a persistent head tilt.

EAR INFECTIONS

We are fortunate that our guys never suffered from a serious ear infection. Cookie had one, but it was quite mild as we caught it early.

MANY DOGS HAVE CHRONIC EAR PROBLEMS

An outer ear infection will cause your dog's ears to smell bad and have brown, yellow or bloody discharge. They will likely scratch at their ears and shake their head excessively.

If the infection is left untreated, it ruptures the eardrum, and moves through the middle ear into the inner ear; the dog might eventually develop a head tilt, loss of balance and start circling. Inner ear infections can also develop through the bloodstream or after an outer ear infection has resolved. In these cases, the part of the ear you can see will look perfectly normal.

ANYTHING THAT AFFECTS THE VESTIBULAR SYSTEM CAN RESULT IN HEAT TILT

Some dogs suffer with what is referred to as an idiopathic vestibular disease.

This is the most common cause of head tilts in older dogs. It is not known what causes the symptoms (head tilt, circling or rolling, abnormal eye movements, and poor balance), but thankfully most dogs with idiopathic vestibular disease recover with simple nursing care over the course of a couple of weeks.

Other causes of vestibular dysfunction and head tilts in dogs include head injury, hypothyroidism, brain inflammation or infection, Cushing's disease, stroke, cancer affecting the ear or brain, anatomic abnormalities within the brain, and even certain drugs.

These are not things you want to leave unchecked.

WHEN IS IT AN EMERGENCY?

Head tilting is an emergency when accompanied by severe pain where you cannot touch or look into your dog's ear.

It may also be an emergency if accompanied by other neurological signs or changes in mentation/behavior.

Bad Odor

Is your dog stinky?

The average dog shouldn't be any stinkier than the average person! In fact, I'd say much less so! And I'm not even taking bad cologne choices into consideration.

Of course, *a bad cologne choice*, at least according to our human standards, can make your dog quite stinky. A good roll in a deer poop or dead fish will certainly do the trick. So would an encounter with a skunk.

Our dogs do their share of covering themselves in odorous substances.

BUT WHAT IF A DOG IS STINKY WITHOUT AN APPARENT REASON?

When I get a whiff of an odor from my dog, I investigate. Every time my dogs stank for an undetermined reason, there was something wrong. Anal gland infection, skin infection, ear infection …

BAD BREATH

Bad breath is most commonly caused by oral disease. Dental issues can cause a lot of pain, tooth loss, destruction of jaw bones, and the associated bacteria can make their way into the bloodstream and cause life-threatening infections in the heart, kidneys, and liver.

Mouth ulcers and melanoma or other tumors of the oral cavity can also cause terrible breath.

Systemic issues, such as kidney failure or diabetes can be the culprit behind bad breath.

SMELLY EARS

Infected ears can generate quite a bit of bad odor. Ear infections can be quite painful, and if left untreated, you're risking serious complications, including deafness, problems associated with the sense of balance, and chronic ear inflammation that requires lifelong management.

Jasmine never had problems with her ears, but I still did a regular "smell check." Cookie had an ear infection once, and I'm checking her ears even more diligently.

SMELLY REAR

Another common source of bad odor is anal sac disease.

Anal sacs produce an incredibly foul smelling liquid which under normal circumstances is only released when a dog defecates or is terrified or excited enough. Cookie once squirted some in excitement. Trust me; you'll know it when you smell it.

You should be able to get through life without ever having the honor of getting acquainted with this smelly essence. If you don't, you better get your dog's rear checked.

Jasmine would get a skin infection from time to time. I was familiar with the smell, and when I caught a whiff, we gave her a medicated bath, and that was usually the end of it. One time I detected a strange smell around her rear. She was also fussing with the area. It didn't have the familiar smell. I couldn't figure out what it was (this was before Cookie honored us with hers). We gave her a bath and everything seemed fine that night. The next day the smell was back. It shouldn't have come this quickly, and it bothered me that it was not the familiar smell. We had her vet check out her hind end, and she had anal sac infection starting.

Impacted glands may release at inappropriate times (like when your dog scoots across the carpet), and the micro-organisms in an infected anal sac can produce quite a pungent odor of their own. Untreated, impacted anal sacs can get infected and abscess. Such things can be incredibly painful.

SMELLY SKIN

Allergies, seborrhea, bacterial or yeast infections can cause all kinds of bad odors. With Jasmine, I have learned to use my nose for early detection of skin in trouble.

The odors associated with skin diseases usually occur in tandem with other symptoms, such as an abnormally greasy coat, itching, flaking, or skin lesions.

It was only once when I didn't catch Jasmine's skin infection soon enough by odor and she actually got to the itchy stage. It was an infection of her hair follicles, and everything smelled and looked just fine until it got nasty in a hurry. That time she did need antibiotics and lost a lot of fur around the area until it all healed.

With any superficial wounds or surgical sites on my dogs, I use my nose daily to check for infection. The nose is an excellent diagnostic tool. Why not use it?

GAS

If your dog produces immense amounts of stinky gas on a regular basis, something is amiss. For the longest time, Jasmine would produce the most foul gas. We saw a vet at least monthly because she also had intermittent diarrhea and other stool issues. Nobody found anything until years later, but she was suffering from inflammatory bowel disease all along.

Cookie sometimes gets bad gas after catching and eating a mouse. Not always; it must be something the mouse ate. Either way, abnormal flatulence can be a sign of a dietary issue or gastrointestinal disease.

HEALTHY DOGS DON'T STINK!

Instead of complaining how stinky your dog is, look for a cause.

WHEN IS IT AN EMERGENCY?

Stinky dog is, clearly, not an emergency. However, if you notice your dog's breath smelling like fruit or nail polish remover, seek prompt veterinary help.

Coughing

While with some other things it's a matter of degree—is the panting/drooling/drinking normal or excessive—a cough is a cough. It doesn't get any more clear-cut than that.

WHEN DO I WORRY?

There is the odd random cough that doesn't mean anything other than something temporarily irritated the throat. When JD decides to bark in the middle of eating something, he often ends up coughing after. Food is supposed to be swallowed, not inhaled.

When our guys are drinking from a bottle they might not always get the water down just right, and it results in a few coughs.

Inhaled irritants, food particles or even pressure from a pulling on a leash can cause a bout of coughing. Such a *random* cough goes away as quickly as it came.

Once Jasmine started coughing after a *bark-off session* with a new dog next door. At first, we thought she had irritated her throat with all that barking. But it wasn't going away, and we ended up at the vets that afternoon.

Her lymph nodes were swollen, and she was running a fever. The vet checked her out and said that it's either lymphoma or infection and that we should try antibiotics first to see what happens.

Scary stuff. You don't spring words like lymphoma at people at random like it was nothing! However, trying the antibiotics first made sense to us, and so we did that. Fortunately, the cough cleared right up, and all was good.

WHAT COULD CAUSE YOUR DOG'S COUGHING?

Coughing is a reflex caused by an irritation in the airways. There is quite a long list of possible reasons why your dog might be coughing

- Respiratory infections (bacterial, viral or fungal)
- Inflammatory or immune conditions (e.g., chronic bronchitis or allergies)
- Parasites
- Heart disease
- Tracheal collapse
- Foreign bodies (e.g., inhaled grass seed or chunks of food)
- Cancer
- Fluid accumulation in or around the lungs
- Trauma

The most common cause of coughing in dogs is kennel cough. It produces a deep, dry, hacking cough that sometimes ends with a gagging sound. It often gets worse with exercise or excitement.

If your dog has been recently boarded, groomed, visited a daycare or other places with a lot of other dogs, kennel cough is a likely suspect.

A harsh, dry cough followed by retching and gagging which lasts for two months or longer could mean chronic bronchitis. It could lead to irreversible damage of the airways. I would never wait this long to see a vet if my dog was coughing. When Jasmine started coughing, I didn't wait to the next day!

Collapsing trachea is a condition that results from weakening of the cartilage in the windpipe. The wall of the windpipe (trachea) narrows as the air tries to travel through. It produces a rather characteristic goose-honk cough. Small, brachycephalic ("smushed face") breeds are particularly susceptible to collapsing trachea.

Parasites, such as heartworms, lungworms, and larvae of some intestinal parasites can also cause coughing.

Enlarged heart or congestive heart failure (CHF) causes fluid to accumulate in or around the lungs which results in coughing. The resulting soft, wet-sounding cough will last for prolonged periods of time, particularly at night during rest.

Young dogs or dogs that have not been vaccinated can come down with canine distemper. Symptoms start with a runny nose and eyes, fever, lack of appetite, and, as you'd guess, coughing. Distemper is included in core vaccinations for a reason. The above symptoms are just the beginning. What follows after that are serious neurological symptoms. Distemper can be fatal, and there is no treatment other than supportive care.

As much as we hate to think about that, cancer can also cause coughing.

Never underestimate coughing.

WHEN IS IT AN EMERGENCY?

If your dog coughs for more than 6 hours, has a hard time breathing, coughs to the point of vomiting, is coughing up blood, or is lethargic, inappetant, or depressed, see your vet immediately.

Excessive Licking

Cats lick themselves all the time; they are big on self-grooming. It's when they stop that you need to worry.

Dogs, though, are not like that. They are mostly happy with their bodies just the way they are.

LICKING IS A DOG'S WAY OF TRYING TO ALLEVIATE DISCOMFORT

Every time Jasmine started licking herself, I went looking for a problem and found one.

When she started licking around her tail, she had a skin infection starting. Caught early enough we could often tackle it with medicated baths. A couple of times it got bad in a hurry, though and needed veterinary attention.

Once, her licking the area around her tail, together with a suspicious smell, alerted me to the start of an anal gland infection.

EVERY TIME IT MEANT SOMETHING WAS GOING ON

When she licked her foot a lot, an infection was starting there. That happened frequently enough that when I heard more than a couple of licks, I'd grab my flashlight and go searching.

Cookie is the same way. Usually, we hardly ever see her licking herself, but when she does, it's typically a boo-boo she acquired running through the bushes and brambles. A bit of betadine is usually all it needs.

WHAT WOULD HAPPEN IF I LEFT IT UNCHECKED, THOUGH?

Some infections can move fast and get nasty in a hurry.

Even if you don't see or hear your dog licking, you can often find evidence in the form of wet fur or bedding.

It was Cookie's licking of her vulva that first alerted me to her dribbling problem. As she could feel the urine dribble, she was trying to clean it up.

MY DOGS NEVER LICK THEMSELVES WITHOUT A REASON

Yes, sometimes licking can be a behavioral issue or even a type of seizure disorder. But I believe that more often than not a physiological reason can be found.

THE FIRST STEP IN DIAGNOSING AND TREATING EXCESSIVE LICKING IS A THOROUGH HEALTH WORK-UP BY YOUR VET

Allergies are a common cause.

Fleas, wounds, insect bites and foreign bodies are right up there as well, with infections close on their tail. But remember, infections are rarely the primary cause.

If a part of the body hurts, such as from arthritis, your dog might lick that area as well. Or there can be a neurological cause, as there was in Jasmine's case.

WHAT IF A DOG EXCESSIVELY LICKS THINGS OTHER THAN THEMSELVES?

A recent study tied excessive licking of surfaces to issues with the digestive tract, including giardiasis, chronic pancreatitis, liver disease, inflammatory bowel disease, and other conditions.

Dental issues, adrenal issues, nervous system issues, all these things can make your dog lick everything within reach like there was no tomorrow.

Dogs don't do anything without a reason. The reason might be fulfilling their needs, communication or to alleviate pain or discomfort.

IT DOESN'T END THERE

Excessive licking not only reflects the level of your dog's discomfort, but it can also cause additional problems from secondary infections to lick granulomas.

I know people who simply put a cone of shame on their dog to stop them from licking themselves. But think how horrible that must feel. Having an itch or pain and not being able to do anything about it. I imagine that's what hell might be like.

The best way to stop your dog's excessive licking is to find and address the cause.

WHEN IS IT AN EMERGENCY?

Excessive licking can help point to emergency situation if a dog is having difficulty giving birth, if there is weakness and abnormal bleeding or vaginal discharge, or if a male dog's penis is exposed and cannot be withdrawn back into the sheath.

Unexplained Weight Loss

Unless it happens rapidly, weight loss is one of the potentially *quiet symptoms* that I find quite scary. If your dog has been overweight, you might welcome that the pounds are coming off.

THERE ARE TWO POTENTIAL PROBLEMS WITH WEIGHT LOSS

When it happens too rapidly, when it's not *on purpose*, or both.

Any unexplained weight loss is a concern. And sometimes things get even more complicated than just that.

One of my friends was trying hard to get her dog to lose some weight. They were struggling with the dog acting as if she was always starved and yet not shedding a pound. Then, finally, yet another diet plan apparently solved both issues, and the weight started coming off. Fast. And then the dog suddenly died from aggressive lymphoma ...

If there is a loss of appetite, vomiting or diarrhea, such weight loss is *explained* but you, clearly, still have a problem to address. See a vet.

When unexplained weight loss comes with lower energy levels or lethargy, skin and coat changes, changes in drinking habits and urination, see a vet. If your dog keeps losing weight in spite of a ravenous appetite, see a vet.

Whenever something is happening that shouldn't, or without a good reason, I see a vet.

A NUMBER OF THINGS CAN CAUSE WEIGHT LOSS

- change in diet
- an inadequate or poor quality diet
- reduced appetite
- maldigestion or malabsorption of nutrients
- metabolic issues
- loss of nutrients such as due to diarrhea, vomiting or renal disease
- increased requirement for calories such as neoplasia

More specifically things such as

- parasites
- dental disease
- liver disease
- kidney disease or failure
- chronic partial GI obstruction
- an intestinal disease such as inflammatory bowel disease (IBD)
- chronic infections
- protein-losing intestinal disorder
- diabetes
- hyperthyroidism
- cancer
- heart disease
- Cushing's disease
- Addison's disease ...

The list of possibilities is quite long.

If your dog is losing weight, the two questions to ask yourself are whether your dog is getting enough calories and whether there have been changes in appetite as well.

To determine whether your dog is getting enough calories, measure what they are being fed and work out if it is appropriate.

There is a big difference between your dog losing weight because they are not so interested in eating and losing weight in spite of being hungry all the time. Those two things have vastly different causes.

WHEN WEIGHT LOSS IS ABOUT SOMETHING ELSE

Sometimes, what you might see as *simple weight loss* can be in fact generalized loss of muscle mass, not just fat. This is particularly a sign of more serious diseases such as kidney failure, liver failure, heart disease, or cancer.

If the bones along your dog's spine and skull become more visible than they used to be, make an appointment with your veterinarian immediately.

WHEN IS IT AN EMERGENCY?

Unexplained weight loss is a progressive issue, and while it calls for veterinary attention, it does not represent an immediate emergency in itself.

Unexplained Weight Gain

This is a tough one. A majority of dogs are already overweight or obese. Most of the time we're not even aware of a problem, particularly when it happens gradually.

THE FIRST STEP IS KNOWING WHAT YOUR DOG'S BODY SHOULD LOOK AND FEEL LIKE

And you can't judge by other dogs of the same breed, not even dog show champions because these days many too are overweight. What it boils down to these days is that if your dog seems too thin to you, they're probably at an ideal weight. Sad but true.

SOME OBJECTIVE MEASURES OF ASSESSING YOUR DOG'S BODY

Can you feel your dog's ribs easily? Does your dog have a visible waistline? Tummy tuck?

If the curves on your dog start disappearing (dogs shouldn't be shaped like tubes!), your dog is putting on some undesired pounds.

"Look how she's beautifully *filling in*."

That's what people kept saying when Jasmine started losing her *youngster, all-legs look*. We were none wiser. After all, she was a Rottweiler - those are supposed to be big, right? Then we adopted Bruin who was huge. Just seeing the two side by side made Jasmine look tiny. And she kept packing the pounds on, *undetected* by either her vet or us.

It wasn't until we were trying to get to the bottom of a completely different problem when her vet finally noticed that she might be chubbier than she should be. And it turned out her thyroid wasn't working properly.

Once treated, the extra weight just melted away.

IF YOU FIND YOUR DOG PUTTING ON SOME EXTRA WEIGHT, ASK YOURSELF WHY

Quite often the answer to weight gain is simple. Too much food, too many treats, wrong food or treats, too little activity ... Be honest with your vet and mainly yourself. If the answer is simply too many bacon bits, the solution is unpleasant but straightforward.

WHAT IF YOU ARE POSITIVE THAT YOUR DOG DOES NOT GET AN EXCESSIVE AMOUNT OF CALORIES?

There is a formula that allows you to calculate how many calories a day your dog needs. If you do want to calculate your dog's energy requirements, the formula and instructions can be found online @ petMD[24].

The next important step is to add up how many calories your dog gets in a day. The tricky part is to calculate EVERYTHING, including any treats, table scraps, or supplements.

But what if your dog gets just the right amount of calories and still gaining weight?

---

24 http://www.petmd.com/blogs/nutritionnuggets/jcoates/2013/aug/how-many-calories-does-dog-need-30849

IF THE ANSWER ISN'T IN THE BOWL, IT IS IN THE BODY

There are a number of medical causes behind weight gain or the appearance of weight gain. It does make sense that metabolic diseases would have a direct impact on weight gain or weight loss.

For me, if my dogs start gaining weight without eating more or exercising less, hypothyroidism is a prime suspect. Low thyroid function leads to a sluggish metabolism. This means that much of the energy consumed gets stored as fat instead of being used by the body to function. That's also why a hypothyroid dog has low energy, difficulty keeping warm and weak immune system.

Cushing's disease is caused by an overproduction of hormones that are involved in protein, carbohydrate, and metabolic regulation. A dog with Cushing's disease will gain weight while their muscles are wasting. The typical potbelly seen with Cushing's disease is caused by fat shifting into the abdomen, weakening of the abdominal muscles and an enlargement of the liver.

Some prescription drugs can cause weight gain.

Large abdominal tumors or fluid retention, such as that seen with some types of heart or liver disease or even some parasites can cause an enlarged belly that has nothing to do with obesity.

WHEN IS IT AN EMERGENCY?

A sudden expansion of the abdomen, particularly paired with signs of pain, agitation and unproductive retching can be signs of a life-threatening condition commonly known as bloat or gastric dilatation volvulus (GDV). This needs immediate medical intervention.

Bloated abdomen can also be a result of internal bleeding, such as from a splenic tumor. This would be accompanied by lethargy, weakness, pale mucus membranes and other signs. This is an emergency.

Shaking or Trembling

I was not even going to write about this. I figured it didn't need to be pointed out as a potentially serious symptom. But I come across enough posts where either dog owners or even vets don't seem to find it worrisome enough, even when other symptoms are present.

YES, MANY SMALL BREED DOGS SHAKE AT THE DROP OF A HAT

My daughter's Chi shakes when she gets excited to see somebody. She'll shake when she's anxious or scared, or when she's cold (and she does get cold easily).

HYPOTHERMIA

Make no mistake, being too cold can be just as dangerous as being too hot. To complicate things further, when a dog gets very cold, the shaking eventually stops. But that's not a good thing. It's a sign that the dog's normal warming mechanisms are shutting down.

If your dog has been out in wet, cold, and/or windy conditions and becomes lethargic, unresponsive, stiff, and/or uncoordinated, they are in trouble and need to get someplace warm and receive medical attention right away.

If you're outside with your dog on a cold day, do watch them carefully.

How much cold a dog can tolerate depends on their size, breed, coat, age, health, what they're used to, and even individual constitution. JD has less tolerance to cold than Cookie does even though he's bigger. He even has less cold tolerance than Jasmine did and she was quite a bit older. So even though they are the same breed, about the same size and both have had the same opportunity to adjust to weather changes, we have to make allowances for the difference.

When it's damp, raining and windy it doesn't even have to be that cold for your dog to develop hypothermia.

WITH SMALL OR ANXIOUS DOGS, THINGS GET TRICKIER

Since some small dogs seem to shake for any ol' reason, how can you tell when to worry?

Personally, unless my dog were shaking from excitement or anticipation, I'd worry. Even though anxiety or fear is not likely to kill your dog on the spot, ongoing or frequent stress will have a negative impact on their health. Plus I simply wouldn't want my dog in situations that stress them out that much.

HYPOGLYCEMIA

Small dogs (especially small breed puppies) are more prone to hypoglycemia, which is low blood sugar. Lethargy and uncontrollable shaking are the signs to watch for. Untreated, hypoglycemia can lead to seizures and even death.

DON'T SHRUG IT OFF

Shaking or trembling can also be a sign of pain, injury, poisoning, kidney disease ... almost anything that makes a dog feel poorly. Especially when other symptoms are present, do not wait to see a vet. It breaks my heart to read online questions such as, "my dog has been vomiting all day, has diarrhea, and it's trembling, what can I do to help him at home?"

It breaks my heart even more when somebody's dog "has been really quiet and weird, trembles and shakes, not eating and barely drinking, barely active, hiding ... took him to the vet twice this week ... the vet told me to monitor him since it doesn't seem like an emergency since he's not vomiting or having diarrhea."

If my dog were shaking or trembling, with or without any other worrisome symptoms, I'd want a definite answer and a plan to help them.

SOME SCARY REASONS BEHIND SHAKING/TREMBLING

- pain
- hypoglycemia
- poisoning
- kidney failure
- inflammatory brain diseases or seizure disorders
- Addisonian crisis
- Distemper
- neurological disorder
- neuromuscular diseases (e.g. myasthenia gravis)
- liver disease leading to hepatic encephalopathy

If my dog was shaking or trembling with the absence of apparent cause of excitement, I'm on the way to a vet.

WHEN IS IT AN EMERGENCY?

Unless I knew that my dog is shaking and trembling as a result of an emotional state, I'd treat it as an emergency.

In Closing

A Word on Pet Health Insurance

My advice on pet health insurance is very simple - get it. The last thing you need when something happens is to have two problems instead of one. Trust me. I've been there and done that.

With Roxy, we did not have enough money to even try to get her diagnosed. With Jasmine, we exhausted all our resources and credit and are still paying off the debt. There is nothing like being able to decide on diagnostics and treatments based on what your dog needs rather than having to work with what you can afford, or bury yourself in debt.

EMERGENCY FUND WON'T CUT IT

Too often I see friends, who had an emergency fund or thought they were otherwise set to take care of unexpected vet bills, watch it blown away in a matter of weeks.

We too had a savings account for Jasmine's medical emergencies. I talked to her vet; we discussed the costs of various possible emergency procedures or surgeries. We had saved five thousand dollars.

The amount was grossly underestimated.

Money ran out in a blink of an eye. Credit was exhausted. Jasmine's veterinary costs added up to $75,000 in five years. That's only counting since she reached the age of five.

WE THOUGHT WE DIDN'T NEED AN INSURANCE

Why shove money down a big corporation's throat when you can put it in a savings account instead, right? Every month we put aside a monthly premium's worth. But just one of Jasmine's medical emergencies came to $12,000.

Let's do a little math. Say you figure your insurance premium would be $150, so you put that aside every month. At that rate, it would take almost seven years to have enough money to cover such an emergency. Is your dog going to wait to have something happen to them? I suppose they better.

What if the emergency bill is going to be even more? What if there is going to be more than one emergency? What if your dog is going to require multiple surgeries or cancer treatment? The advances in veterinary medicine are awesome and allow our dogs to overcome medical situations they couldn't have in the past. But they come at a *price*.

Here are some examples of treatment costs published by Trupanion[25].

Patellar luxation	Required surgery and pain medications	$4,012
Legg-Perthes disease	Surgery and long-term medications	$6,466
Glaucoma	Long-term medications and surgery	$5,805
Portacaval shunt	Required surgery and medication for a period of time	$6,267
Hip dysplasia	Long-term medications and surgery	$7,815
Diabetes	Long-term medications and blood work	$10,496
Ectropion	Required surgical correction	$2,050

---

25 http://trupanion.com/canada/pet-insurance/actual-claims

Fragmented coronoid process	Long-term medications and surgery	$7,006
Fever of unknown origin and pneumonia	Required emergency surgery and hospitalization	$8,294
Ingestion of foreign body	Required surgery on cat to remove a swallowed hair pin	$2,964
Gastric dilation volvulus (GDV)	Required surgery to turn stomach back to normal and staple it to the wall of chest	$3,525
Parvo gastroenteritis	Liquid and medication for inflammation of the stomach and intestines	$5,084
Stick lodged in between molars	Surgery required	$1,656
Cruciate ligament tear	Surgery to repair torn right hind ACL and post-op complication	$5,439
Cancer (sarcoma)	Chemotherapy	$5,351
Hit by car and fractured pelvis	Emergency surgery/span	$3,717
Acute liver failure	Emergency center treatment	$5,453
Seizures	MRI and medications for seizures	$1,984

How many months you'd have to be saving to cover any of those? And I tell you those are by far not the highest bills you can run into.

Watching our veterinary bills mount, we quickly got insurance for JD.

He has been quite healthy, but even his medical costs added up, last with his mast cell tumor. We could have probably have taken care of it for less, but we are only comfortable going all out to do what is best for the dog.

Even with JD being always relatively healthy, his bills added up. And that is not counting routine preventive stuff.

We insured Cookie right after we adopted her. Cookie, bless her sweet soul, wouldn't be where she is if it wasn't for having her insured.

Do you think the premiums are stiff? Yeah, I agree. But wait for the bills.

Maybe your dog will be the lucky one who never gets hurt or sick. Are you willing to bet their lives on it?

I'm presently helping a friend raise funds for treatment of her dog. I know the desperate feeling too well. Funds are gone, and if their dog is to live and have any chance for decent quality of life, the expense is going to be substantial.

What do you do? You do whatever you can. And if you're lucky you get to do what it takes.

Or just have an insurance.

Having an emergency fund or savings account is a beautiful idea. But from where I stand it's never going to be enough if things really go wrong.

Epilogue

I did not write "Symptoms to Watch for in Your Dog" as a reference book; it is a "wake up and smell the waffles" book.

I cannot overstate the importance of being a health advocate for your dog. Yes, it involves *more work*. Starting with being able to tell when your dog's health is in trouble, and ending with *working the case* to a reasonable conclusion. To goal is restoring your dog to health, effective management if health cannot be restored, or at least a full understanding of what is going on and what to expect. At the end of the day, it will always be worth it.

I wish somebody had told me this before I learned it the hard way. It took me five years of endless vet visits before I finally realized that perhaps something was amiss. It took me five years to start questioning things and demand answers that would result in solutions.

Fortunately, by the time the worst disaster struck, I was up to the task. If I weren't, that's when Jasmine's life would have ended. At the age of five and a half.

I knew her condition was an emergency. We took her to the ER immediately when that became clear. But then, were I to accept the emergency vet's diagnosis and recommendations, that would have been it. Only because by then I knew to question things that didn't make sense I had Jasmine transferred to a teaching hospital for a second opinion instead of *putting her down* as the ER recommended based on their [wrong] diagnosis. Jasmine recovered from that medical disaster, and others, and lived over four more happy years.

Today, I leave no stone unturned, no question unanswered. Something doesn't make sense? Treatment isn't working? Rest assured I wouldn't leave things be until I get either a solution or at least an explanation.

Appendix: Normal Vital Signs

Vital signs include temperature, resting heart rate, resting pulse rate, resting respiratory rate, capillary refill time and color of mucous membranes[26].

Because dogs come in all shapes and sizes, the normal ranges are rather broad, and it is important that you learn what normal vital signs are for your dog.

NORMAL AVERAGE VITAL SIGNS RANGES

TEMPERATURE	37.5 - 39.2 °C (99.5 - 102.5°F
RESTING HEART RATE	60 - 140 beats/minute
RESTING PULSE RATE	60 - 140 beats/minute
RESTING RESPIRATORY RATE	15 - 35 breaths/minute
CAPILLARY REFILL TIME	1 - 2 seconds
MUCOUS MEMBRANES	pink

---

26 http://www.vetstreet.com/dr-marty-becker/what-is-normal-dog-temperature-heart-rate-and-respiration

TEMPERATURE

When taking your dog's temperature, don't forget that the only reliable way is with a rectal thermometer. Neither you or your dog might like this, but if you need reliable information, this is the way to get it. Don't forget to lube it! Remember, very high or very low temperature are an emergency! *(pg. 57)*

HEART RATE

Place your hand over the left side of your dog's rib cage, just behind the elbow. Count the number of beats for 15 seconds and multiply by 4.

PULSE RATE

To check your dog's pulse rate, find your dog's femoral artery on the inside of your dog's thigh. Count the number of beats for 15 seconds and multiply by 4.

Pulse rate can differ from the heart rate if the heart is not producing enough pressure, such as with some arrhythmias.

RESPIRATORY RATE

Check by counting your dog's chest movements for 15 seconds and multiply by 4. High respiratory rate can be due to stress, but it can also mean pain, anemia, congestive heart failure or respiratory issues. A dog with markedly decreased respiratory rate can be in shock.

MUCOUS MEMBRANES AND CAPILLARY REFILL TIME

To check your dog's mucous membranes *(pg. 99)* and capillary refill time, lift the upper lip. Check for color. Then press a finger against the gum, release, then measure how long it takes before the color returns to normal.

Resources

RECOMMENDED BOOKS

Speaking for Spot, Dr. Nancy Kay
Your Dog's Best Health, Dr. Nancy Kay
Dog Owner's Home Veterinary Handbook, Debra M. Eldredge
Your Dog: The Owner's Manual, Dr. Marty Becker
What's Wrong with My Dog?, Dr. Jake Tedaldi
First Aid for Pets, Dr. Joanna Paul

RECOMMENDED WEBSITES

www.veterinarypartner.com
www.petmd.com
www.peteducation.com

To talk to a vet online try
www.pawbly.com
www.justanswer.com
www.vetlive.com
www.vetondemand.com

Acknowledgments

So many people helped me to get to where I am today, I am grateful to every one of them. Here are just some who deserve special recognition.

Dr. Rae Worden, Jasmine's vet, who has been there with us the whole way, putting up with me, answering my questions, and always working with me for the best benefit of my dogs. He's the one who first showed me what a veterinarian could be.

All the vets we've worked with, past and present. Both those who were great and those who failed my dogs. They all had been a blessing because they all taught me something.

Dr. Joanna Paul for working with me on this book with care and dedication, and being a great friend.

Dr. Krista Magnifico for lending her expertise and helping with the book as well as always being there for me when I need help with my dogs.

All my online veterinary friends who helped me with my learning, brainstorming and finding answers, particularly Dr. Daniel Beatty, Dr. Patrick Mahaney, Dr. Justine Lee, and Dr. Nancy Kay who's fantastic book *Speaking for Spot* I wish was available when I was going through the steepest learning curve with Jasmine.

All my online veterinary friends who participated on the book and my blog, namely Dr. Julie Buzby, Dr. Daniel Beatty, Dr. Keith Niesenbaum, Dr. Rae Worden, Dr. Anna Coffin, Dr. Patrick Mahaney, Dr. Nancy Kay, and Dr. Krista Magnifico.

All the wonderful people at Vet-Stem who had been amazing and provided great help and support both with Jasmine's and Cookie's treatments. Special thanks to Kristi Moore Hauta who has always gone out of her way to be there for us.

All my dog-loving friends who have always been there for me when I needed them.

Gabrielle Scanlon, a copyeditor extraordinaire, who helped to polish the language and structure.

Howard VanEs of Let's Write Books, Inc, for helping me with the publishing of this book.

And last but not least I'd like to thank my husband, the driver. He's always had faith in my learning ability and judgment even when I didn't.

About the Author

Jana Rade is a devoted fur-mom and dog health advocate extraordinaire. And she's on a mission to help you. Jana used her intuition, passion, knowledge and resourcefulness to compile a wealth of practical information that you can use to help you navigate just about any ailment your dog may experience. This volume is the result of years of incredible and fastidious research into pet health, nutrition, training, behavior and all things dog. Jana has hobnobbed with veterinarians, whom she now counts among her friends, and scoured the globe for dawgie specialists. At first it was to help her own dogs. But she soon realized that many others were asking the same kinds of questions she had asked on her journey. In her book, Jana shares her experience and insights accumulated with her own dogs, as well as the dogs of family members and friends, who's journeys she had the privilege to be part of.

Even with gravely ill dogs, the signs can sometimes be deceptively subtle. Knowing when to seek help can improve your dog's health, quality of life, and sometimes be the difference between the life and death.

WHERE YOU CAN FIND JANA

Dawg Business blog: https://dawgbusiness.blogspot.com
Dog Health Issues Support Group: https://www.facebook.com/groups/doghealthissues
Twitter: @DawgBlogger
Facebook: https://www.facebook.com/DawgBlogger